CliffsNotes™

W9-BAQ-962

The Great Gatsby

By Kate Maurer, Ph.D.

IN THIS BOOK

- Learn about the Life and Background of the Author
- Preview and Introduction to the Novel
- Explore themes, character development, and recurring images in the Critical Commentaries
- Examine in-depth Character Analyses
- Acquire an understanding of the novel with Critical Essays
- Reinforce what you learn with CliffsNotes Review
- Find additional information to further your study in the Cliffs-Notes Resource Center and online at www.cliffsnotes.com

Houghton Mifflin Harcourt
Boston   New York

About the Author
Kate Maurer received her Ph.D. in English from Marquette University and is currently an Assistant Professor of Composition and English at the University of Minnesota Duluth.

Editor
Gary Carey, M.A., University of Colorado

Consulting Editor
James L. Roberts, Ph.D., Department of English, University of Nebraska

Publisher's Acknowledgments
Senior Project Editor: Michael Kelly
Acquisitions Editor: Greg Tubach
Copy Editor: Greg Pearson
Glossary Editors: The editors and staff at Webster's New World Dictionaries
Editorial Administrator: Michelle Hacker
Editorial Assistant: Brian Herrmann

Composition
Wiley Indianapolis Composition Services

CliffsNotes™ *The Great Gatsby*

Copyright © 2000 Houghton Mifflin Harcourt
Library of Congress Control Number: 00-104430
ISBN: 978-0-7645-8601-9
Printed in the United States of America
DOC 30 29 28 27 26 25 24 23 22
4500644401
1O/RV/QW/QY/IN

Note: If you purchased this book without a cover, you should be aware that this book is stolen property. It was reported as "unsold and destroyed" to the publisher, and neither the author nor the publisher has received any payment for this "stripped book."

For information about permission to reproduce selections from this book, write to trade.permissions@hmhco.com or to Permissions, Houghton Mifflin Harcourt Publishing Company, 3 Park Avenue, 19th Floor, New York, New York 10016.

www.hmhco.com

LIMIT OF LIABILITY/DISCLAIMER OF WARRANTY: THE PUBLISHER AND AUTHOR HAVE USED THEIR BEST EFFORTS IN PREPARING THIS BOOK. THE PUBLISHER AND AUTHOR MAKE NO REPRESENTATIONS OR WARRANTIES WITH RESPECT TO THE ACCURACY OR COMPLETENESS OF THE CONTENTS OF THIS BOOK AND SPECIFICALLY DISCLAIM ANY IMPLIED WARRANTIES OF MERCHANTABILITY OR FITNESS FOR A PARTICULAR PURPOSE. THERE ARE NO WARRANTIES WHICH EXTEND BEYOND THE DESCRIPTIONS CONTAINED IN THIS PARAGRAPH. NO WARRANTY MAY BE CREATED OR EXTENDED BY SALES REPRESENTATIVES OR WRITTEN SALES MATERIALS. THE ACCURACY AND COMPLETENESS OF THE INFORMATION PROVIDED HEREIN AND THE OPINIONS STATED HEREIN ARE NOT GUARANTEED OR WARRANTED TO PRODUCE ANY PARTICULAR RESULTS, AND THE ADVICE AND STRATEGIES CONTAINED HEREIN MAY NOT BE SUITABLE FOR EVERY INDIVIDUAL. NEITHER THE PUBLISHER NOR AUTHOR SHALL BE LIABLE FOR ANY LOSS OF PROFIT OR ANY OTHER COMMERCIAL DAMAGES, INCLUDING BUT NOT LIMITED TO SPECIAL, INCIDENTAL, CONSEQUENTIAL, OR OTHER DAMAGES. FULFILLMENT OF EACH COUPON OFFER IS THE RESPONSIBILITY OF THE OFFEROR.

Trademarks: Houghton Mifflin Harcourt, Cliffs, CliffsNotes, CliffsAP, CliffsComplete, CliffsTestPrep, CliffsQuickReview, CliffsNote-a-Day, and related trade dress are trademarks or registered trademarks of Houghton Mifflin Harcourt and/or its affiliates in the United States and other countries and may not be used without written permission. All other trademarks are the property of their respective owners. Houghton Mifflin Harcourt is not associated with any product or vendor mentioned in this book.

Table of Contents

How to Use This Book

This CliffsNotes study guide on F. Scott Fitzgerald's *The Great Gatsby* supplements the original literary work, giving you background information about the author, an introduction to the work, a graphical character map, critical commentaries, expanded glossaries, and a comprehensive index, all for you to use as an educational tool that will allow you to better understand *The Great Gatsby*. This study guide was written with the assumption that you have read *The Great Gatsby*. Reading a literary work doesn't mean that you immediately grasp the major themes and devices used by the author; this study guide will help supplement your reading to be sure you get all you can from Fitzgerald's *The Great Gatsby*. CliffsNotes Review tests your comprehension of the original text and reinforces learning with questions and answers, practice projects, and more. For further information on F. Scott Fitzgerald and *The Great Gatsby*, check out the CliffsNotes Resource Center.

CliffsNotes provides the following icons to highlight essential elements of particular interest:

Reveals the underlying themes in the work.

Helps you to more easily relate to or discover the depth of a character.

Uncovers elements such as setting, atmosphere, mystery, passion, violence, irony, symbolism, tragedy, foreshadowing, and satire.

Enables you to appreciate the nuances of words and phrases.

Don't Miss Our Web Site

Discover classic literature as well as modern-day treasures by visiting the CliffsNotes Web site at www.cliffsnotes.com. You can obtain a quick download of a CliffsNotes title, purchase a title in print form, browse our catalog, or view online samples.

You'll also find interactive tools that are fun and informative, links to interesting Web sites, tips, articles, and additional resources to help you, not only for literature, but for test prep, finance, careers, computers, and the Internet, too. See you at www.cliffsnotes.com!

LIFE AND BACKGROUND OF THE AUTHOR

The following abbreviated biography of F. Scott Fitzgerald is provided so that you might become more familiar with his life and the historical times that possibly influenced his writing. Read this Life and Background of the Author section and recall it when reading Fitzgerald's *The Great Gatsby*, thinking of any thematic relationship between Fitzgerald's work and his life.

Personal Background

The Early Years

September 24, 1896 marks the birth date of F. Scott Fitzgerald, one of the foremost twentieth century American writers. Born in St. Paul, Minnesota, young Scott was christened Francis Scott Key Fitzgerald, in honor of his second cousin three times removed, Francis Scott Key, the author of the National Anthem. His father, Edward, brought breeding, charm, and a sense of elegance to the family, although as a businessman, he experienced only marginal financial success. Fitzgerald's mother, Mollie McQuillan, was the daughter of an Irish immigrant who made a fortune in the wholesale grocery business. Although she came from a family of means, she had little interest in society life, except as it regarded her son's future. The family lived comfortably on the outskirts of the city's most fashionable residential neighborhood, Summit Avenue, thanks largely to the generosity of the McQuillan family. Although the Fitzgeralds lived just blocks from the city's most elegant and wealthy families, they were not considered rich and therefore were perched precariously on the community's social hierarchy. They possessed what some critics have come to call "a certain genteel shabbiness." It seems likely much of Fitzgerald's interest in society life began in his youth in Minnesota when he would play and associate with the rich children of the neighborhood—dancing, sailing, swimming, sledding—all the time knowing he was never entirely a part of their society.

The Fitzgeralds lived in Minnesota on and off during Scott's youth. When his father's business folded in 1897, the elder Fitzgerald took a job the following year as a salesman for Procter and Gamble, consequently moving his family to New York, first to Buffalo, then Syracuse, and then back to Buffalo. He was fired from his job in 1908, and just months before Scott's twelfth birthday, the family returned to St. Paul where the McQuillan family still lived. From that point, the Fitzgeralds essentially lived off the McQuillan family fortune. Although Scott would call St. Paul home from 1908 to 1922, he was often not there. Rather, he spent much of that time at boarding school, at Princeton University, in the army, and in New York City.

Prep School and College

Although Edward and Mollie Fitzgerald did not mingle much in the society life of their community, they saw to it that Scott met the right people. He attended the prep school and dancing classes where the elite sent their children. In 1908, Fitzgerald entered the St. Paul Academy where he was received with mixed welcome (many of the students apparently thought he was too arrogant). He excelled in debate and athletics, pushing himself continually. In 1909, "The Mystery of the Raymond Mortgage" was published in the school magazine *Now & Then*, marking the first time Fitzgerald was in print. He would publish three more stories in the next two years. He would also begin writing plays while still a student at St. Paul.

In 1911, however, due largely to Scott's less than stellar scholastic record, his parents sent him to the Newman School, a Catholic prep school in Hackensack, New Jersey. Here he met Fr. Sigourney Fay who would serve as a mentor, encouraging him to develop his talents and pursue his dreams of personal achievement and distinction. During the years at Newman, Fitzgerald published three stories in the school literary magazine, helping him to realize that despite his interest in athletics, he was more successful in literary endeavors.

In 1913, Fitzgerald entered Princeton University. Again, he would not prove himself a top scholar, although his literary achievements began to grow. He wrote scripts and lyrics for the Triangle Club musicals and contributed to Princeton publications. By 1917, Fitzgerald was on academic probation and, given graduation looked unlikely, he joined the army, commissioned as a second lieutenant in the infantry. He continued to write, however, and in 1918, *The Romantic Egotist* was rejected by Charles Scribner's Sons, with a request for resubmission upon revision.

Marriage and Work

In 1918, while assigned to Camp Sheridan, near Montgomery, Alabama, the course of his life changed forever. The 22-year-old Scott met and fell in love with then 18-year-old debutante Zelda Sayre. Zelda, youngest daughter of an Alabama Supreme Court judge, refused marriage, however, until Scott could support her in the manner to which she was accustomed. After being discharged from the army in February 1919, Fitzgerald moved to New York and took up work with an advertising agency, hoping to earn enough money so he and Zelda could be married. By June of 1919, Zelda had tired of waiting for Scott to earn his fortune and broke their engagement.

During the summer of 1919, Fitzgerald quit the ad business to return to St. Paul to rewrite *The Romantic Egotist*. In September of the same year noted Scribner's editor Maxwell Perkins accepted *This Side of Paradise*, as the novel was now called, for publication. One week after its publication, Scott and Zelda were married in New York. The novel meant instant success for the young author and pushed the newlyweds into the limelight. Together, Scott and Zelda became synonymous with life in the 1920s. In many regards, the Fitzgeralds' lifestyle read like something out of one of Scott's novels. Stories of their drinking, dancing, and extravagant lifestyle surround the couple. Over the years, they traveled between the United States and Europe (especially France) extensively, becoming (at least for a while) part of "The Lost Generation" of American expatriates in Paris. In 1921, Zelda gave birth to the couple's only child, a daughter named Frances Scott Fitzgerald (known as Scottie).

Despite their celebrated status, the Fitzgeralds' domestic life was plagued with hardships. Throughout their marriage, the two went through periods of heavy alcohol consumption. Although Fitzgerald wrote sober, he drank more and more frequently and excessively. Drinking was also a factor in the Fitzgeralds' frequent fights. In some scholars' opinions, stories of Scott's drinking earned him the reputation for an "irresponsible writer," which kept him from being taken seriously by the literary community. The Fitzgeralds' marriage was also plagued by financial difficulties. Although *This Side of Paradise* did well, the follow-up novel did not meet the same success. In order to maintain their extravagant lifestyle, Scott spent much time working on short stories that ran in widely distributed magazines.

Another major obstacle to the Fitzgeralds' domestic happiness came to light in 1930, when Zelda experienced her first of three mental breakdowns. Although she had been troubled during much of their marriage, by 1930, Zelda's condition had worsened such that she was institutionalized. This breakdown left her in various care facilities in France and Switzerland from April 1930 to September 1931. She suffered a second breakdown less than six months later in February 1932, resulting in four months' hospitalization in the United States. Zelda's third breakdown, which occurred in January 1934, left her institutionalized until her death in a fire at her last hospital in 1948.

Although Scott remained married to Zelda until the end, her mental illness redefined their marriage. Zelda required more care than Scott could give, and so he worked hard to keep her comfortably hospitalized (in fact, many of the couple's later debts resulted from Zelda's institutionalization). Scott eventually met and fell in love with Sheilah Graham, a movie columnist, with whom he spent the last few years of his life. Graham's support and encouragement helped put Scott's stalling career back onto the path of creative productivity.

Major Works

Although Scott is known for his novels, his literary talents ran much deeper. Over the course of his career, Fitzgerald wrote four complete novels, while a fifth, partially completed at the time of his death, was published posthumously. *This Side of Paradise* (1920) marked the beginning of Fitzgerald's career as a novelist and was built largely around experiences and observations made while at Princeton. While also writing short stories, Fitzgerald completed *The Beautiful and Damned* (1922), a book first serialized in *Metropolitan Magazine*. *The Great Gatsby* (1925), the novel for which Fitzgerald has become most well known, met only limited success upon its publication. In the years since, it has gone on to become nearly synonymous with Fitzgerald and life in the Roaring 20s. Fitzgerald worked on his fourth novel, *Tender is the Night* (1934), sporadically for almost ten years after publication of *The Great Gatsby*. Despite favorable reviews, the novel sold even more poorly than *The Great Gatsby*. At the time of his death in 1940, Fitzgerald was working on *The Last Tycoon* (1941), a novel based upon his experiences in Hollywood. About half the novel was completed at the time of his death, and, according to some literary critics, *The Last Tycoon* quite likely could have been his greatest critical success had it been completed.

Aside from his novels, Fitzgerald amassed a considerable collection of short stories, composing over 150. The Fitzgeralds' lifestyle was expensive, and frequently, short stories brought in much needed money. Beginning in 1919, Fitzgerald's works were frequently published in national publications such as *The Smart Set*, *The Saturday Evening Post*, *Metropolitan Magazine*, *The American Mercury*, *Liberty*, *Scribner's Magazine*, and *Esquire*. He would also publish three collections of short stories during his lifetime: *Flappers and Philosophers* (1920), *Tales of the Jazz Age* (1922), and *All the Sad Young Men* (1926).

In addition to his novels and short stories, at three distinct points in his career Fitzgerald earned his living as a screenwriter in Hollywood. His first job was in 1927, when he worked for United Artists for only a few months. He returned to Hollywood again in the fall of 1931 to work for Metro-Goldwyn-Mayer until the following spring. Fitzgerald made his third and final trip to Hollywood in 1937, drawn there out of dire financial necessity created by Zelda's institutionalization. Fitzgerald signed a six-month contract with MGM Studios at the rate of $1,000 per week. His contract was renewed for another year at the rate of $1,250 per week. In December of 1938, however, in keeping with the sort of luck that seemed to plague Fitzgerald, the contract was not renewed. Fitzgerald stayed in Hollywood, however, and between 1939 and 1940 he freelanced with most of the major studios (Paramount, Universal, Twentieth Century-Fox, Goldwyn, and Columbia) while writing his final novel.

At the time of his death in 1940, Fitzgerald had slipped into relative obscurity. His personal life was chaotic and his literary reputation fragile. Fitzgerald's death, sadly, was not unlike Gatsby's. Despite having once been the golden boy of the Jazz Age, upon his death, many of his obituaries were condescending, capitalizing on his personal hardships. Not one of his books remained in print and every indication suggested he was on his way into obscurity. However, after World War II, interest in his work began to grow. By the 1960s, he had risen from the dustbin to secure a place among the great twentieth century American authors. In the time since, interest in Fitzgerald has remained consistently strong. Together with Zelda, his personal life has become a part of the American landscape, linked forever with the youthful exuberance of the 1920s. Professionally, his works provide a valuable voice for exploring themes of ambition, justice, equity, and the American dream—themes that are still current—affording him with a well-deserved place in the American literary canon.

INTRODUCTION TO THE NOVEL

The following Introduction section is provided solely as an educational tool and is not meant to replace the experience of your reading the work. Read the Introduction and A Brief Synopsis to enhance your understanding of the work and to prepare yourself for the critical thinking that should take place whenever you read any work of fiction or nonfiction. Keep the List of Characters and Character Map at hand so that as you read the original literary work, if you encounter a character about whom you're uncertain, you can refer to the List of Characters and Character Map to refresh your memory.

Introduction

The Great Gatsby, published in 1925, is hailed as one of the foremost pieces of American fiction of its time. It is a novel of triumph and tragedy, noted for the remarkable way its author captures a cross-section of American society. In *The Great Gatsby* Fitzgerald, known for his imagistic and poetic prose, holds a mirror up to the society of which he was a part. The initial success of the book was limited, although in the more than 75 years since it has come to be regarded as a classic piece of American short fiction. In 1925, however, the novel served as a snapshot of the frenzied post-war society known as the Jazz Age, while today it provides readers with, among other things, a portal through which to observe life in the 1920s. Part of Fitzgerald's charm in *The Great Gatsby*, in fact, is his ability to encapsulate the mood of a generation during a politically and socially crucial and chaotic period of American history.

To understand Fitzgerald's genius more fully, one must be aware of the politics that underlie the story. To remove the story from its full historical context is to do it a grave injustice. The novel, published in 1925, explores life in the early- to mid-1920s. Politically speaking, this was a time of growth and prosperity, as well as a time of corruption. World War I, the first war of its kind anyone had ever known, had ended in 1919. When Warren G. Harding assumed the presidency in 1920, one of his goals was to bring the country back to business as usual. However, this proved to be a difficult task because Harding's administration was plagued by scandal and corruption, as well as opposition mounted by both unions and organized crime.

After WWI ended, Harding's administration targeted business as a means of rebuilding the country. What this entailed, however, included undermining striking laborers and largely siding with management in labor dispute issues over such things as minimum wage, unions, child labor, and so on. In addition to favoring management in labor disputes, Harding and his successor, Calvin Coolidge, enacted tax legislation that benefited the wealthy more so than any other group. In addition, because of administrative policy decisions, industries such as agriculture, textiles, and certain types of mining suffered greatly, and as a result, cities grew as people moved to urban areas to make a living. Many of them, however, remained trapped in a purgatory of sorts, looking for a better life but unable to get it, not unlike the people in *The Great Gatsby's* valley of ashes.

Economically, the 1920s boasted great financial gain, at least for those of the upper class. Between 1922 and 1929, dividends from stock rose by 108 percent, corporate profits increased by 76 percent, and personal wages grew by 33 percent. Nick Carraway's journey to the East to make his fortune in the bond business is not entirely unfounded. Largely because of improvements in technology, productivity increased while overall production costs decreased, and the economy grew. All this would come to a grinding halt, however, with the stock market crash of 1929, sending the U.S. into the greatest depression it has ever known. Fitzgerald, of course, couldn't have forecasted the crash, but in *The Great Gatsby*, he does suggest, on one level, that society was living in excess and without curbing its appetite somewhat, ruin was just around the corner.

The commercial growth of the 1920s resulted in rampant materialism, such as that chronicled in *The Great Gatsby*. As people began to have more money, they began to buy more. In turn, as people began to buy more, profits grew, more goods were manufactured, and people earned more money, thereby enabling the economic growth cycle. People began to spend their money on consumer goods—cars, radios, telephones, and refrigerators—at a rate never before seen. People also began to spend time and money on recreation and leisure. Professional sports began to grow in popularity, and movies and tabloid newspapers gained a foothold on America, helping everyone to share, in one way or another, in the growing materialism that categorized the Jazz Age.

In addition to economics, Fitzgerald takes other national issues into consideration in *The Great Gatsby*. For example, in Chapter 1, Tom has an intense dislike for outsiders. Later, other characters, including Nick, refer negatively to immigrants who live in the community of West Egg. Although to modern readers the comments and allusions may seem to lack motivation, such is not the case. Immigration to America was at its peak in the late nineteenth and early twentieth centuries. Although immigration waned during the war years, by June of 1921, immigration had returned again to pre-war levels (800,000 people between June of 1920 and June of 1921) and organized labor began lobbying against immigrants, whom they believed were taking away jobs from American citizens. Business leaders and various special interest groups also began to worry about the influx of immigrants, citing anti-American political fanaticism as a likely problem. In response, Congress passed a series of restriction bills and laws, setting quotas that limited the number of immigrants allowed in a particular year (164,000 in 1924 and

1925; 150,000 after July 1, 1927). The quota was entirely discriminatory, particularly to people from southern and eastern Europe and from Asia. Although readers may not like what Fitzgerald's characters imply, there is certainly a historical basis behind it.

Another aspect of *The Great Gatsby* that has historical roots centers on the Eighteenth Amendment to the Constitution: prohibition. Enacted in 1919 (and ultimately repealed in 1933), this amendment made it illegal for anyone to manufacture, sell, or transport liquor of any sort. Millions of Americans hailed this amendment as a moral advance, curbing America's growing penchant for immorality and all the vices that went (in their eyes) hand in hand with drunkenness. Despite the millions who supported prohibition, millions also broke the law and drank the outlawed liquor. Not surprisingly, when the illegal liquor business became lucrative, organized crime stepped in to meet the demand. Manufacturing and distributing alcohol were big businesses during the years of prohibition and helped make the fortunes of the *nouveaux riches* (newly rich) found within Fitzgerald's novel, including Meyer Wolfsheim and Gatsby himself. An understanding of prohibition also helps explain why Fitzgerald puts such an emphasis on drinking within the novel.

Although political issues underlie *The Great Gatsby*, so, too, do social issues. In many ways, Fitzgerald's Jazz Age characters are a fairly honest representation of what could be found in the social circles of the country's younger generation. Many of the men in *The Great Gatsby* had served in WWI, and like their real-life counterparts, they returned from the war changed. They found the ideas and attitudes waiting for them at home to be representative of an outmoded way of thinking, and so they rebelled. The women at home, too, found post-war America to be too constrictive for their tastes. Many women had entered the workforce when the men went to war and were unwilling to give up the by-products of their employment—social and economic freedom— when the men returned from the war. In addition, the Nineteenth Amendment, enacted in 1920, gave women the right to vote, making their independence even more necessary. In the 1920s, young men and women (including Fitzgerald himself) refused to be content maintaining the status quo, and so they openly and wholeheartedly rebelled.

Socially, the 1920s marked an era of great change, particularly for women. In a symbolic show of emancipation, women bobbed their hair, that one great indicator of traditional femininity. To compliment their more masculine look, women also began to give up wearing corsets, the restrictive undergarment intended to accentuate a woman's hips, waist, and breasts, as if to reinvent themselves, according to their own rules. Other things women did that were previously unheard of included smoking and drinking openly, as well as relaxing formerly rigid attitudes toward sex. Fitzgerald picks up on the social rebellion of his peers particularly well in *The Great Gatsby*. He shows women of all classes who are breaking out of the molds that society had placed them into. Myrtle, for instance, wishes to climb the social ladder, and so she is determined to do so at all costs. Daisy attempts to break away from the restrictive society in which she was raised, yet she cannot make the break entirely and so she falls back into the only thing she knows: money. Jordan Baker, too, is an emancipated woman. She passes time as a professional golfer, a profession made possible largely because of the social and economic progress of the 1920s.

Part of what makes Fitzgerald's novel such a favorite piece is the way he is able to analyze the society of which he was also a part. Through his characters, he not only captures a snapshot of middle- and upper-class American life in the 1920s, but also conveys a series of criticisms as well. Through the characterization in *The Great Gatsby*, Fitzgerald explores the human condition as it is reflected in a world characterized by social upheaval and uncertainty, a world with a direct underlying historical basis. By emphasizing social groupings and how they do or do not interact with each other (see the Critical Essays section in this Note for further explorations), Fitzgerald establishes a sense of urgency. The Jazz Age society so clearly shown in *The Great Gatsby* is, in effect, on a very dangerous course when people like Tom, Daisy, and Jordan are at the top of the ladder, working hard to ensure no one else climbs as highly as they. Through Gatsby, Fitzgerald demonstrates the enterprising Jazz Ager, someone who has worked hard and profited from listening and responding to the demands of the society. Unfortunately, despite his success, Gatsby (and all of the people he represents) is never able to capture his elusive dreams. Fitzgerald's story, although a fiction, is informed by reality, helping to make it one of the most treasured pieces of early twentieth century American fiction.

A Brief Synopsis

The Great Gatsby is a story told by Nick Carraway, who was once Gatsby's neighbor, and he tells the story sometime after 1922, when the incidents that fill the book take place. As the story opens, Nick has just moved from the Midwest to West Egg, Long Island, seeking his fortune as a bond salesman. Shortly after his arrival, Nick travels across the Sound to the more fashionable East Egg to visit his cousin Daisy Buchanan and her husband, Tom, a hulking, imposing man whom Nick had known in college. There he meets professional golfer Jordan Baker. The Buchanans and Jordan Baker live privileged lives, contrasting sharply in sensibility and luxury with Nick's more modest and grounded lifestyle. When Nick returns home that evening, he notices his neighbor, Gatsby, mysteriously standing in the dark and stretching his arms toward the water, and a solitary green light across the Sound.

One day, Nick is invited to accompany Tom, a blatant adulterer, to meet his mistress, Myrtle Wilson, a middle-class woman whose husband runs a modest garage and gas station in the valley of ashes, a desolate and run-down section of town that marks the convergence of the city and the suburbs. After the group meets and journeys into the city, Myrtle phones friends to come over, and they all spend the afternoon drinking at Myrtle and Tom's apartment. The afternoon is filled with drunken behavior and ends ominously with Myrtle and Tom fighting over Daisy, his wife. Drunkenness turns to rage when Tom, in one deft movement, breaks Myrtle's nose.

Following the description of this incident, Nick turns his attention to his mysterious neighbor, who hosts weekly parties for the rich and fashionable. Upon Gatsby's invitation (which is noteworthy because rarely is anyone ever invited to Gatsby's parties—they just show up, knowing they will not be turned away), Nick attends one of the extravagant gatherings. There, he bumps into Jordan Baker, as well as Gatsby himself. Gatsby, it turns out, is a gracious host, but yet remains apart from his guest—an observer more than a participant—as if he is seeking something. As the party winds down, Gatsby takes Jordan aside to speak privately. Although the reader isn't specifically told what they discuss, Jordan is greatly amazed by what she's learned.

As the summer unfolds, Gatsby and Nick become friends, and Jordan and Nick begin to see each other on a regular basis, despite Nick's conviction that she is notoriously dishonest (which offends his sensibilities because he is "one of the few honest people" he has ever met). Nick and Gatsby journey into the city one day and there Nick meets Meyer Wolfsheim, one of Gatsby's associates and Gatsby's link to organized crime. On that same day, while having tea with Jordan Baker, Nick learns the amazing story that Gatsby told her the night of his party. Gatsby, it appears, is in love with Daisy Buchanan. They met years earlier when he was in the army but could not be together because he did not yet have the means to support her. In the intervening years, Gatsby made his fortune, all with the goal of winning Daisy back. He bought his house so that he would be across the Sound from her and hosted the elaborate parties in the hopes that she would notice. It has come time for Gatsby to meet Daisy again, face-to-face, and so, through the intermediary of Jordan Baker, Gatsby asks Nick to invite Daisy to his little house where Gatsby will show up unannounced.

The day of the meeting arrives. Nick's house is perfectly prepared, due largely to the generosity of the hopeless romantic Gatsby, who wants every detail to be perfect for his reunion with his lost love. When the former lovers meet, their reunion is slightly nervous, but shortly, the two are once again comfortable with each other, leaving Nick to feel an outsider in the warmth the two people radiate. As the afternoon progresses, the three move the party from Nick's house to Gatsby's, where he takes special delight in showing Daisy his meticulously decorated house and his impressive array of belongings, as if demonstrating in a very tangible way just how far out of poverty he has traveled.

At this point, Nick again lapses into memory, relating the story of Jay Gatsby. Born James Gatz to "shiftless and unsuccessful farm people," Gatsby changed his name at seventeen, about the same time he met Dan Cody. Cody would become Gatsby's mentor, taking him on in "a vague personal capacity" for five years as he went three times around the Continent. By the time of Cody's death, Gatsby had grown into manhood and had defined the man he would become. Never again would he acknowledge his meager past; from that point on, armed with a fabricated family history, he was Jay Gatsby, entrepreneur.

Moving back to the present, we discover that Daisy and Tom will attend one of Gatsby's parties. Tom, of course, spends his time chasing women, while Daisy and Gatsby sneak over to Nick's yard for a moment's privacy while Nick, accomplice in the affair, keeps guard. After the Buchanans leave, Gatsby tells Nick of his secret desire: to recapture the past. Gatsby, the idealistic dreamer, firmly believes the past can be recaptured in its entirety. Gatsby then goes on to tell what it is about his past with Daisy that has made such an impact on him.

As the summer unfolds, Gatsby and Daisy's affair begins to grow and they see each other regularly. On one fateful day, the hottest and most unbearable of the summer, Gatsby and Nick journey to East Egg to have lunch with the Buchanans and Jordan Baker. Oppressed by the heat, Daisy suggests they take solace in a trip to the city. No longer hiding her love for Gatsby, Daisy pays him special attention and Tom deftly picks up on what's going on. As the party prepares to leave for the city, Tom fetches a bottle of whisky. Tom, Nick, and Jordan drive in Gatsby's car, while Gatsby and Daisy drive Tom's coupe. Low on gas, Tom stops Gatsby's car at Wilson's gas station, where he sees that Wilson is not well. Like Tom, who has just learned of Daisy's affair, Wilson has just learned of Myrtle's secret life—although he does not know who the man is—and it has made him physically sick. Wilson announces his plans to take Myrtle out West, much to Tom's dismay. Tom has lost a wife and a mistress all in a matter of an hour. Absorbed in his own fears, Tom hastily drives into the city.

The group ends up at the Plaza hotel, where they continue drinking, moving the day closer and closer to its tragic end. Tom, always a hot-head, begins to badger Gatsby, questioning him as to his intentions with Daisy. Decidedly tactless and confrontational, Tom keeps harping on Gatsby until the truth comes out: Gatsby wants Daisy to admit she's never loved Tom but that, instead, she has always loved him. When Daisy is unable to do this, Gatsby declares that Daisy is going to leave Tom. Tom, though, understands Daisy far better than Gatsby does and knows she won't leave him: His wealth and power, matured through generations of privilege, will triumph over Gatsby's newly found wealth. In a gesture of authority, Tom orders Daisy and Gatsby to head home in Gatsby's car. Tom, Nick, and Jordan follow.

As Tom's car nears Wilson's garage, they can all see that some sort of accident has occurred. Pulling over to investigate, they learn that Myrtle Wilson, Tom's mistress, has been hit and killed by a passing car that never bothered to stop, and it appears to have been Gatsby's car. Tom, Jordan, and Nick continue home to East Egg. Nick, now disgusted by the morality and behavior of the people with whom he has been on friendly terms, meets Gatsby outside of the Buchanans house where he is keeping watch for Daisy. With a few well-chosen questions, Nick learns that Daisy, not Gatsby, was driving the car, although Gatsby confesses he will take all the blame. Nick, greatly agitated by all that he has experienced during the day, continues home, but an overarching feeling of dread haunts him.

Nearing dawn the next morning, Nick goes to Gatsby's house. While the two men turn the house upside down looking for cigarettes, Gatsby tells Nick more about how he became the man he is and how Daisy figured into his life. Later that morning, while at work, Nick is unable to concentrate. He receives a phone call from Jordan Baker but is quick to end the discussion—and thereby the friendship. He plans to take an early train home and check on Gatsby.

The action then switches back to Wilson, who, distraught over his wife's death, sneaks out and goes looking for the driver who killed Myrtle. Nick retraces Wilson's journey, which placed him, by early afternoon, at Gatsby's house. Wilson murders Gatsby and then turns the gun on himself.

After Gatsby's death, Nick is left to help make arrangements for his burial. What is most perplexing, though, is that no one seems overly concerned with Gatsby's death. Daisy and Tom mysteriously leave on a trip, and all the people who so eagerly attended his parties, drinking his liquor and eating his food, refuse to become involved. Even Meyer Wolfsheim, Gatsby's business partner, refuses to publicly mourn his friend's death. A telegram from Henry C. Gatz, Gatsby's father, indicates he will be coming from Minnesota to bury his son. Gatsby's funeral boasts only Nick, Henry Gatz, a few servants, the postman, and the minister at the graveside. Despite all his popularity during his lifetime, in his death, Gatsby is completely forgotten.

Nick, completely disillusioned with what he has experienced in the East, prepares to head back to the Midwest. Before leaving, he sees Tom Buchanan one last time. When Tom notices him and questions him as to why he didn't want to shake hands, Nick curtly offers, "You know what I think of you." Their discussion reveals that Tom was the impetus behind Gatsby's death. When Wilson came to his house, he told Wilson that Gatsby owned the car that killed Myrtle. In Tom's mind, he had helped justice along. Nick, disgusted by the carelessness and cruel nature of Tom, Daisy, and those like them, leaves Tom, proud of his own integrity.

On the last night before leaving, Nick goes to Gatsby's mansion, then to the shore where Gatsby once stood, arms outstretched toward the green light. The novel ends prophetically, with Nick noting how we are all a little like Gatsby, boats moving up a river, going forward but continually feeling the pull of the past.

List of Characters

Jay Gatsby The protagonist who gives his name to the story. Gatsby is a newly wealthy Midwesterner-turned-Easterner who orders his life around one desire: to be reunited with Daisy Buchanan, the love he lost five years earlier. His quest for the American dream leads him from poverty to wealth, into the arms of his beloved, and, eventually, to death.

Nick Carraway The story's narrator. Nick rents the small house next to Gatsby's mansion in West Egg and, over the course of events, helps Gatsby reunite with Daisy (who happens to be Nick's cousin). Nick's Midwestern sensibility finds the East an unsettling place, and he becomes disillusioned with how wealthy socialites like the Buchanans lead their lives.

Daisy Buchanan Beautiful and mesmerizing, Daisy is the apex of sociability. Her privileged upbringing in Louisville has conditioned her to a particular lifestyle, which Tom, her husband, is able to provide her. She enraptures men, especially Gatsby, with her diaphanous nature and sultry voice. She is the object of Gatsby's desire, for good or ill, and represents women of an elite social class.

Tom Buchanan Daisy's hulking brute of a husband. Tom comes from an old, wealthy Chicago family and takes pride in his rough ways. He commands attention through his boisterous and outspoken (even racist) behavior. He leads a life of luxury in East Egg, playing polo, riding horses, and driving fast cars. He is proud of his affairs and has had many since his marriage. Myrtle Wilson is merely the woman of the moment for Tom.

Pammy Buchanan Toddler daughter of Tom and Daisy Buchanan. Little mention is made of her, and she represents the children of the Jazz Agers. She has very little parental contact, yet the reader is always vaguely aware of her presence.

Jordan Baker Professional golfer of questionable integrity. Friend of Daisy's who, like Daisy, represents women of a particular class. Jordan is the young, single woman of wealth, admired by men wherever she goes. She dates Nick casually but seems offended when he is the first man not to fall for her charms. Although she is savvy, she comes off as somewhat shallow in her approach to life.

Myrtle Wilson Married lover of Tom Buchanan. Myrtle serves as a representative of the lower class. Through her affair with Tom she gains entre into the world of the elite, and the change in her personality is remarkable. She conducts a secret life with Tom, wherein she exhibits all the power and dominance she finds lacking in her everyday life. She eventually suffers a tragic end at the hands of her lover's wife.

George Wilson Myrtle's unassuming husband. He runs a garage and gas station in the valley of ashes and seems trapped by his position in life. Eventually, he finds out about his wife's double life and his response to it helps drive her to her death. Distraught at what happens, Wilson becomes Fitzgerald's way of expressing the despair prevalent in the seemingly trapped lower-middle class.

Catherine Sister of Myrtle Wilson who is aware of her sister's secret life and willing to partake of its benefits.

Meyer Wolfsheim Gatsby's business associate and link to organized crime. A professional gambler, Wolfsheim is attributed with fixing the 1919 World Series. Wolfsheim helped build Gatsby's fortune although the wealth came through questionable means.

Michaelis George Wilson's restaurateur neighbor who comforts Wilson after Myrtle is killed. One of the few charitable people to be found in the novel.

Ewing Klipspringer Convivially known as Gatsby's "boarder." Klipspringer is a quintessential leech, a representative of the people who frequented Gatsby's partys.

Dan Cody Worldly mentor of Jay Gatsby. Cody took Gatsby under his wing when Gatsby was a young man and taught him much about living adventurously and pursuing dreams.

Henry C. Gatz Father of Jay Gatsby. Comes from the Midwest to bury his son. Gatz serves as a very tangible reminder of Gatsby's humble heritage and roots.

Character Map

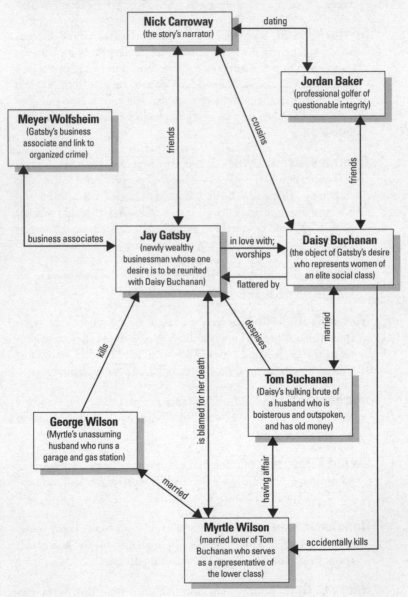

CRITICAL COMMENTARIES

The sections that follow provide great tools for
supplementing your reading of *The Great Gatsby*. First, in
order to enhance your understanding of and enjoyment
from reading, we provide quick summaries in case you
have difficulty when you read the original literary work.
Each summary is followed by commentary: literary
devices, character analyses, themes, and so on. Keep in
mind that the interpretations here are solely those of the
author of this study guide and are used to jumpstart your
thinking about the work. No single interpretation of a
complex work like *The Great Gatsby* is infallible or
exhaustive, and you'll likely find that you interpret
portions of the work differently from the author of this
study guide. Read the original work and determine your
own interpretations, referring to these Notes for
supplemental meanings only.

Chapter 1

Summary

As *The Great Gatsby* opens, Nick Carraway, the story's narrator, remembers his upbringing and the lessons his family taught him. Readers learn of his past, his education, and his sense of moral justice, as he begins to unfold the story of Jay Gatsby. The narration takes place more than a year after the incidents described, so Nick is working through the filter of memory in relaying the story's events. The story proper begins when Nick moves from the Midwest to West Egg, Long Island, seeking to become a "well-rounded man" and to recapture some of the excitement and adventure he experienced as a soldier in WWI. As he tries to make his way as a bond salesman, he rents a small house next door to a mansion which, it turns out, belongs to Gatsby.

Daisy Buchanan, Nick's cousin, and her husband, Tom, live across the bay in the fashionable community of East Egg. Nick goes to visit Daisy, an ephemeral woman with a socialite's luminescence, and Tom, a brutish, hulking, powerful man made arrogant through generations of privilege, and there he meets Jordan Baker, the professional golfer and a girlhood friend of Daisy's. As the foursome lounge around the Buchanans' estate, they discuss the day's most pressing matters: the merits of living in the East, what to do on the longest day of the year, reactionary politics, and other such shallow topics. When Tom takes a phone call, Jordan informs Nick that Tom's mistress is on the phone. Tom, known for his infidelities, makes no pretense to cover up his affairs. As Tom and Daisy work to set up Nick and Jordan, they seize the opportunity to question Nick about his supposed engagement to a girl back home. Nick reassures them there is no impending marriage, merely a series of rumors that cannot substitute for truth.

Upon returning home that evening, as he is sitting outside, Nick notices a figure emerging from Gatsby's mansion. Nick's initial impulse is to call out to Gatsby, but he resists because Gatsby "gave a sudden intimation that he was content to be alone." While watching Gatsby, Nick witnesses a curious event. Gatsby, standing by the waterside, stretches his arms toward the darkness, trembling. This gesture seems odd to Nick because all he can make out is a green light, such as one finds at the end of a dock, across the Sound. Looking back at the mysterious figure Nick realizes that Gatsby has vanished.

Commentary

Fitzgerald opens his novel by introducing Nick Carraway, the story's narrator. Nick has, by his own admission, come "back from the East last autumn," jaded and embittered by his experiences there. The reader knows immediately that the story has already taken place and that Nick is telling it to us through the filter of time. He is distanced from the events at hand and is recounting them by way of memory. It is imperative that readers trust him, then, because time can distort memories, and the reception to the story hinges largely on his impartiality and good judgment.

Character Insight

As a means of establishing faith in the narrator, Fitzgerald carefully develops Nick and positions him both within and without the dramatic situation, creating a dynamic and powerful effect. From the very beginning, even before learning about Gatsby, "the man who gives his name to this book," Fitzgerald gives details about Nick. In his "younger and more vulnerable years" (suggesting he is older and wiser now), his father gave him advice that he has carried with him ever since: "Whenever you feel like criticizing any one . . . just remember that all the people in this world haven't had the advantages that you've had." The implications are strong: Nick comes from at least a middle class family that values a sense of moral justice. In this way, the reader is encouraged to trust Nick and to believe in his impartiality and good judgment; a biased narrator will make the narrative reactionary, not honest, so stressing his good judgment is crucial. To ensure that readers don't think Nick is superhuman in his goodness, however, Fitzgerald gives him a mortal side. Nick's reservation of judgment about people is carefully calculated ("snobbish," as he even says) and even Nick, the rational narrator, can be pushed too far. His tolerance has a limit, and it is the challenge to this limit that forms the basis of the book at hand.

As the chapter continues, more of Nick's background is discussed: the way in which he was raised and his moral character. Nick continues to sell himself, informing the reader that he is an educated man, having graduated from New Haven, home of Yale University. He comes from "prominent, well-to-do people in this Middle Western city for three generations." This seemingly simple detail is crucial. It qualifies Nick to be part of the action which he will unfold—a tale of socialites, money, and privilege—while also keeping him carefully apart. He has come from the Midwest, which for Fitzgerald is a land of perceived morality. Nick has moved East, and disgusted, returns to the Midwest. The reader knows that Nick is not only upset over the action that he will unfold, but he is downright offended by the moral rancor of the situation. Readers, wanting to believe in their own moral fortitude, find themselves siding with Nick, trusting him to exercise the same sound judgment they themselves would exercise.

Theme

The story begins. It is 1922, and Nick has moved East to seek his fortune as a bond salesman, a booming, thriving business that, he supposes, "could support one more single man." Fitzgerald introduces one of the novel's key themes, wealth, upon Nick's arrival in the East. Nick settles in West Egg rather than East Egg, living in a small rental house adjacent to Gatsby's mansion, paying $80 per month rather than the $3000 to $4000 per month for which the houses around him rent. This detail immediately encourages readers to see the difference between the "haves" and the "have nots." Although both Eggs have beautiful mansions, East Egg is home to "old money," people whose families have had great wealth for generations. West Egg, although also home to the rich, is home to "new money," people whose wealth was recently earned, as well as to working class people such as Nick. On another level, the delineation between the Eggs can also be a metaphorical representation of the sensibilities of people from the Eastern and Western parts of the United States.

The story's first adventure, and the one that comprises a large portion of Chapter 1, is Nick's visit with his cousin, Daisy Buchanan, and her husband, Tom, at their mansion in East Egg. The visit not only introduces the other characters crucial to the story, but it also presents a number of themes that will be developed in various ways throughout the novel. Daisy and Tom appear in stark contrast to the image of Nick: Whereas he is relatively industrious (after all, he came East by himself to make his fortune rather than staying home and doing what is expected of him), the Buchanans live in the lap of luxury. Arriving at the mansion, Nick is greeted by Tom, dressed in riding clothes. Tom is an impressive figure, dressed for a sport linked closely with people of wealth and means ("effeminate swank" as Nick calls it). He stands boldly, with "a rather hard mouth," "a supercilious manner," "two shining arrogant eyes," and speaks with "a touch of paternal contempt." Clearly, Tom is not a gentle and sensitive man. Rather, he is harsh and powerful, caring little for social equality and protocol. He has rank and privilege and that's the way he wants to keep it. The first words out of his mouth—"I've got a nice place here"—bring home his inbred superiority as well. As the story unfolds, Tom serves as a foil to Gatsby, marking a striking contrast from Gatsby's newly found wealth and dreamy nature.

Fitzgerald sets the women, Daisy and her friend Jordan Baker, in a dreamlike setting, emphasizing their inability to deal with reality. Both young women, dressed entirely in white (suggesting purity or, in contrast, a void of something such as intellectualism), are engulfed by the expansiveness of the room in which they are sitting. In one of Fitzgerald's many evocative and imagistic passages, he notes how both women's dresses are "rippling and fluttering as if they had just been blown back in after a short flight around the house." As Tom shuts the windows and the breeze dissipates, "the two young women ballooned slowly to the floor." Hardly could a more languid image be created. These are not people who concern themselves with eking out a living.

As the scene unfolds and they begin conversation, the superficial nature of these socialites becomes even more pronounced. Daisy speaks in a voice known for its ability to draw people in (a voice that Gatsby later defines as having money in it). She appears she hasn't a care in the real world, with fulfilling her own whims. The conversation at the dinner furnishes a few key details: This collection of East Eggers focuses on matters of little practical or significant importance and when they do speak of what they perceive to be weighty and meritorious matters, the parts of themselves they reveal are not flattering. For instance, when Tom chooses to discuss politics, he reveals himself not just as one who discriminates against people on the basis of class (a *classicist*), but also a racist. He comes from a land of privilege and unlike Nick, doesn't subscribe to the adage about withholding judgment because not everyone has had the same advantages. For Tom, all that matters is that *he* has had advantages; everything he does in the book comes from his selfish attempt to keep himself in a certain strata while denying anyone else access, even his mistress, who is introduced in Chapter 2.

Theme

Another key theme introduced at the dinner party is that of societal expectation. Much of *The Great Gatsby* centers on appearances and the rift between who or what one is and who or what society wishes or expects. Fitzgerald has already given a sense of this dichotomy when first introducing the Buchanans: They're expected to be gracious and generous, but instead seem shallow and superficial. Just as Nick prepares to head home for the night, Daisy calls for him to wait because she "forgot to ask [him] something, and it's important." "We heard you were engaged to a girl out West," Daisy begins. Nick denies the rumor flatly: "It's a libel. I'm too poor" (curiously, his response also brings home another of the story's key themes—wealth—and as the story unfolds, money and marriage are at its heart). Daisy insists, "But we heard it . . . we heard it from three people, so it must be true." Nick, aware of what they are referring to, reveals that the hometown gossip over his engagement was, in fact, part of what brought him East; he had "no intention of being rumored into marriage." Nick, strong enough to withstand social pressure, becomes a striking contrast to the people introduced throughout the rest of the story who will, time after time, succumb to the power of suggestion, oftentimes to dire ends.

Nick, strangely "confused and a little disgusted" as he drives home, finds an equally curious site waiting for him when he arrives at his house. While sitting outside, he sees Gatsby's silhouette as he crosses to the water. Nick, seeing something in Gatsby's behavior that suggests he wishes to be alone, remains in the shadows watching. Gatsby proceeds to the water and stretches out his arms toward the water, trembling. Nick, looking to see what Gatsby was gesturing to, finds nothing but "a single green light, minute and far away, that might have been the end of a dock." This single green light has gone on to become one of the most famous symbols in all of American literature (see the Chapter 5 commentary for an explanation). It appears here, in Chapter 5, and again at the book's end. The light marks Daisy's house— Gatsby's gesture toward it, as the later chapters show, is a gesture of love.

Glossary

(Here and in the following sections, difficult words and phrases are explained.)

New Haven City in southern Connecticut; home to Yale University.

The Great War World War I

Midas and Morgan and Maecenas Midas, in Greek Myth, the king of Phrygia granted the power of turning everything that he touches into gold; J.P. Morgan (1837–1913), U.S. financier; Gaius Clinius Maecenas (70–8 BC), Roman statesman and patron of Horace and Virgil.

Goddard's The Rise of the Colored Empires an allusion to Theodore Lothrop Stoddard's *The Rising Tide of Color Against White World Supremacy* (1920).

Chapter 2

Summary

Chapter 2 begins with a description of the valley of ashes, a desolate and forsaken expanse of formerly developed land that marks the intersection of the city with the suburbs. In addition to its desolate feel and uniform grayness, this forlorn area is home to a decaying billboard that calls attention to itself. Depicted on the advertisement are the Eyes of Doctor T.J. Eckleburg, which are described as "blue and gigantic— their retinas are one yard high." It was in the valley of ashes that Nick first meets Tom's mistress, Myrtle Wilson. The two men are headed to New York when Tom insists they get off the train in order for Nick to "meet [his] girl."

The two men proceed to a car repair garage owned by George Wilson, a "spiritless man" who is also Myrtle's husband. Tom chats briefly with Wilson about business matters. Myrtle, a sensuous, fleshy woman in her middle thirties, joins the men. Tom quietly informs her he wishes to see her and so she arranges to meet them shortly, leaving her husband under the pretense of visiting her sister in New York. While on their way to Tom and Myrtle's apartment, Myrtle spies a man selling dogs and insists on having one. Once at the apartment, Myrtle phones her sister, Catherine, and her friends, the McKees, to join the party. The six people spend the afternoon in a haze of drunkenness. As the afternoon wears on and she becomes increasingly intoxicated, Myrtle becomes more and more outspoken about her situation in life, her marriage, her impassioned first meeting with Tom, and finally, Tom's marriage. Upon mentioning Daisy's name, Myrtle becomes enraged, shouting "Daisy" at the top of her lungs. Tom, incensed by this outburst, lashes out with his open hand and breaks Myrtle's nose in one "short deft movement." The party enters into a downward spiral and the guests take their departure. The chapter ends with Nick seeing Mr. McKee home and then heading home himself.

Commentary

Whereas Chapter 1 ended with the mysterious Gatsby reaching out to his dream in the night, Chapter 2 opens with a striking contrast. Nick tells us about a stretch of land lying "about half way between West Egg and New York" which is so desolate that it is merely a "valley of ashes—a fantastic farm where ashes grow like wheat into the ridges and hills and grotesque gardens; where ashes take the forms of houses . . . [and] with a transcendent effort, of men who move dimly and already crumbling through the powdery air." As the geographic midpoint between what is in effect the suburbs and the city, the valley of ashes, a dreamless, colorless place bound on one side by a putrid river, is home to the sorts of people that the wealthy citizens of the Eggs and the sophisticated people of the city are content to overlook.

The ashen quality of the community is reflected in every element— including the dilapidated billboard of Doctor T.J. Eckleburg, perhaps the second most memorable image in *The Great Gatsby* (following closely behind the green light at the end of the dock). In many regards, the mysterious eyes hovering above the valley of ashes serve as spiritual force. They are, as George Wilson says, the eyes of God. The faceless eyes hover over all that goes on in the book—a book decidedly void of traditional spirituality. The eyes, in this sense, represent the lack of Godliness in the lives of the characters, and by extension, the society on which Fitzgerald comments. The 1920s, for a certain sect of society, were characterized by an increasing freedom and recklessness—Gatsby's parties are perfect testament to the growing debauchery of the upper class. Through Doctor Eckleburg's sign, Fitzgerald indicates that although people are turning away from traditional (established) morality and rules of socially acceptable behavior, neglecting to tend to their spiritual side, the eyes of God continue to watch all that passes. Even though God's image may become increasingly removed from daily life (just as the face surrounding Eckleburg's enormous eyes has faded and disappeared), His eyes continue to witness all that passes. Through the eyes the reader has an implicit call to action, reconnecting with a lost spiritual connection.

After Nick and Tom get off the train (notice how Tom orders Nick around and announces what it is they are going to do; these are clear indicators of Tom's nature and continue to mark him as the story continues), they proceed to George Wilson's repair garage. Much can be learned about Wilson, as well as everyone trapped in the valley of ashes, through the brief exchange. There is little about Wilson to indicate he will ever be anywhere but the desolate wasteland of the valley. He is common, "blond," "spiritless," "anæmic" and only faintly handsome. His business totters on the brink of failure, and he seems ignorant of what goes on around him. It is unlikely that he is, in Tom's elitist words, "so dumb he doesn't know he's alive," but he does seem trapped by an unnamable force.

Character Insight

Myrtle Wilson appears in striking contrast to her husband. Although she does not possess the ethereal qualities of Daisy, in fact, she appears very much of the earth, she does possess a decided sensuality, as well a degree of ambition and drive that is conspicuously absent in her husband. After a few attempts at social niceties (showing that Myrtle, despite being trapped in a dead-end lifestyle, aspires in some sense to refinement and propriety), Nick and Tom leave, with the understanding that Myrtle will soon join them to travel into the city to the apartment that Tom keeps for just such purposes. It is worth noting, however, that Myrtle rides in a different train car from Tom and Nick, in accordance with Tom's desire to pander, in this small way, to the "sensibilities of those East Eggers who might be on the train." The irony runs deep, giving a greater sense of Tom's character. He is bold about his affair, not worrying that Daisy knows, but he sees the need to put up a pretense on the train, as if that one small gesture of discretion makes up for all the other ways in which he flaunts his affairs.

As soon as the group arrives in New York, Myrtle shows herself to be not nearly as nondescript as is her husband. She is, however, far from refined, despite how she may try. Her purchases at a newsstand (two tabloid-like publications), as well as the way she painstakingly selects just the right taxicab (lavender with gray upholstery) suggests that she is concerned with appearance and fashion, aspiring to be part of the jet-set that she reads about in her magazines and which, she thinks, she can gain entrée to through her wealthy lover.

At the apartment in New York, after "throwing a regal homecoming glance around the neighborhood," Myrtle undergoes a transformation. By changing her clothes she leaves behind her lower-class trappings, and in with donning new clothes she adopts a new personality. She invites her sister and some friends to join the afternoon's party, but her motivation for doing so goes beyond simply wanting to enjoy their company. Her intent is largely to show off what she has gained for herself through her arrangement. It is irrelevant to Myrtle that what she has gained comes through questionable means; clearly, for her (and Tom, too), the morality of infidelity is not an issue. Her affair with Tom allows her to gain something she wants—money and power—and therefore it can be justified.

As Nick describes, when Myrtle changes her clothes, she exchanges her earlier "intense vitality" (clearly a positive and refreshing attribute) for "impressive hauteur" (a decidedly unappealing quality invoking Nick's respect and disgust simultaneously). While entertaining, Myrtle comes across as perceiving herself to be superior, although that isn't hard to do, given the people with whom she surrounds herself. The McKees, for instance, are trying desperately to be accepted by the upper class, but are really shallow, dull people. Mr. McKee, despite his attempts to be seen as an artist, is conventional (even boring) in his photography. He skill is technical, at best, rather than artistic, as he would have people believe, as evidenced by the completely unoriginal titles he gives his photos: 'Montauk Point—the Gulls' and 'Montauk Point—the Sea.'

As Myrtle has more and more to drink, she becomes increasingly belligerent, ordering people about and assuming a false sense of social superiority, casually offering derogatory comments about various types of people—in many ways, mirroring Tom's sense of social superiority. By this point she sees herself not only as superior to her guests, she is Tom's equal.

All this changes, however, when Tom brutally reminds her of her place in his life. After bringing up Daisy's name, Tom and Myrtle stand "face to face, discussing in impassioned voices whether Mrs. Wilson had any right to mention Daisy's name." Myrtle, made bold by the whiskey, begins to shout Daisy's name while Tom, exhibiting the brute force Nick has known he was capable of since first meeting him, quickly hits Myrtle with his open hand, breaking her nose.

Theme

The shocking violence of this incident is calculated and underscores a nastier side of life that most people would like to ignore. Through Tom's assault, Fitzgerald not only demonstrates more about Tom and his callousness toward humanity, but also suggests a hidden side to the Jazz Age. Although most people associate good times and carefree abandon with the reverie of the 1920s, Fitzgerald suggests a much darker side. Tom is a decidedly unpleasant man, held in check by very few rules. The reader must wonder, if he is capable of this sort of violence, what else is he capable of? In just the second chapter of the book, Fitzgerald is already showing the seedy side to a supposedly charmed life. The incident piques the reader's interest, shocking and appalling as it is, making the reader wonder to what depths this society will fall—in the book and in real life, as well.

Theme

It is appropriate to briefly explore the tones of homoerroticism that underlie the party at Tom and Myrtle's. Catherine, Myrtle's sister who is "said to be very beautiful by people who ought to know" (again introducing the notion of rumors and truth, as well as the idea that a certain portion of society has the right to set standards for other portions), speaks in couched terms about her travels and living arrangements with "a girl friend at a hotel." Although this does not, in any way, indicate that Catherine is a lesbian, it does introduce the *possibility*. As Fitzgerald shows by the afternoon's party, anything can happen. It's a wild time—people, particularly the trendy people, are eager to break established boundaries. It is not unlikely that they would challenge established social mores, as well. Nick, himself, has an encounter shrouded in mystery in this chapter, which again hints at challenging the accepted sexual morality of the time—homosexuality was not commonly spoken of at this time in history.

At the end of the chapter, Nick says that after he sees McKee home, after a curious use of ellipses by Fitzgerald, he "was standing beside his bed and he was sitting up between the sheets, clad in his underwear, with a great portfolio in his hands." Fitzgerald very purposely skirts the issue, dropping hints, but no concrete evidence, and leaves the reader to ponder the possibility of a sexual encounter between the two men. Some may argue that looking at this chapter's homoerroticism is pointless; if the author had wanted to focus on it, he would have made it more pronounced in the text. What these critics overlook, however, is the possibility that Fitzgerald is hinting at it, just as the society of which he was a part hinted at it. By refusing to make the book's underlying homoerroticism pronounced, he is mirroring the refusal of society at large to acknowledge a lifestyle choice that was socially unacceptable in most circles. The hints of homoerroticism also bring into focus the debauchery which marks *The Great Gatsby*. The 1920s, Fitzgerald suggests, was not just a time of challenging social boundaries. It was also a time of changing sexual—and even spiritual—boundaries.

Glossary

anæmic having anemia, an illness of the blood resulting in paleness and generalized weakness; also can mean anyone lacking vigor or vitality; lifelessness.

J.D. Rockefeller (1839–1937); U.S. industrialist and philanthropist.

Simon Called Peter Robert Keable's best-selling fiction work from 1922.

hauteur disdainful pride; haughtiness; snobbery.

Kaiser Wilhelm ruler of Germany, 1871–1918. Remember, the U.S. had not long prior fought WWI (1914–1918) wherein the Allies (Great Britain, Russia, France, the United States., Italy, Japan, and so on) fought against the Central Powers (Germany, Austria, Hungary, and others).

kike a Jew: a vulgar term of hostility and contempt.

Chapter 3

Summary

Nick's attentions again turn to Gatsby in Chapter 3. Gatsby, in the summer months, was known far and wide for the extravagant parties he threw in which "men and girls came and went like moths among the whisperings and the champagne and the stars." During the weekend, people flocked to his house for his parties, as well as to use his pool, his boats, his car, and so on. His gatherings were lavishly catered (serving two complete dinners), boasting not just a small combo of musicians, but a whole orchestra. The guests enjoyed themselves, flirting and dancing, until the wee hours of the morning.

After seeing these parties from afar, Nick is invited by Gatsby by a handwritten note to join in the festivities. Nick is one of the few to have actually been invited. The others simply arrive, knowing only that there will be a party and they won't be turned away. At the party, Nick tries to find Gatsby, but has no luck. No one can tell him where Gatsby is, suggesting that they, themselves, didn't know the host. As Nick mills around the party, he encounters Jordan Baker and the two of them two mingle around, inadvertently gathering rumors about Gatsby, including that he had once killed a man. After several glasses of champagne, Nick begins a conversation with a fellow who is, unbeknownst to him, Gatsby himself. Later, Gatsby takes Jordan Baker aside to speak with her privately. What they discuss is not revealed, but Jordan passes along that it is "the most amazing thing."

Not wanting the reader to think his summer was composed merely of the three events outlined in the book's first three chapters, Nick interjects that much more happened to him, although it largely entailed working, dating casually, and dining at the Yale Club. His affinity for New York has been growing throughout the summer as he begins to appreciate its "enchanted metropolitan twilight" and how everyone hurried "toward gayety." Nick meets up with Jordan Baker in mid-summer and as the two begin to see more of each other, Nick begins to look upon her with "a sort of tender curiosity." He realizes, though, that Jordan is "incurably dishonest." In fact, the reason Nick remembered her name initially is that she had once been accused of cheating in a golf tournament. Despite Jordan's downfalls, she intrigues Nick, although he ends the chapter by touting his own cardinal virtue, claiming modestly, "I am one of the few honest people that I have ever known."

Commentary

Literary Device

Chapter 3 is, in many ways, like Chapter 2, moving from one party to another, encouraging the juxtaposition of the two events. Tom's party and Gatsby's party are quite different, although in some ways alike, encouraging the reader to explore in what ways the two men are also similar. The purpose of Chapter 3 is, also like Chapter 2, to provide essential background, although this time it is Gatsby who is introduced. By inserting the chapter about Tom, Fitzgerald has effectively held off introducing the story's main character, helping to build an air of mystery around him, not unlike the mystery that Nick and the others initially associate with him, and by keeping the reader from meeting Gatsby, Fitzgerald links the reader even more closely to Nick. However, the information is sketchy—later chapters help to round out the picture of him: who he is and where he comes from.

Nick tells of Gatsby's parties, elaborate and grand affairs that attract entertainers, socialites, and even ordinary people. Gatsby is a perfect host, generous and hospitable. In fact, he is courteous to the point of being taken advantage of. People routinely come to his house for the parties, but also to use his boats, his plane, his cars, and so on. Gatsby must not mind all his guests, however, because every weekend continues in the same patterns of excess and opulence as he provides his guests with only the finest food, drink, and entertainment.

Nick, living next door to Gatsby, has been observing the parties at a distance, as a casual observer, but in Chapter 3 he is officially invited to attend one. As he moves from being a spectator to being a participant, Nick is able to provide an informed view of not only what goes on at Gatsby's parties, but also what the partygoers themselves are like. When Nick reveals that he is one of the few invited guests at the party, this little detail tells quite a lot: It signals that in some yet unexplained way, Nick is set apart from the typical party guest. Despite living next door to Gatsby, he has never succumbed to the urge to crash one of the parties (which would have been easy enough to do, given the way in which people come and go from Gatsby's affairs). Perhaps it is Nick's Midwestern roots and their implied propriety that keep him at a distance, but regardless, his sense of decorum shows brightly throughout this scene, helping readers see him as a character with integrity.

Having Nick at Gatsby's party provides an unprecedented chance to peer into the lives of the seemingly well-to-do people who attend. The impression is not very appealing. It turns out that the glamorous and glib party guests are, in fact, quite shallow. Nick says that they "conducted themselves according to the rules of behavior associated with amusement parks," again stressing the carefree, stereotypical roaring '20s atmosphere. Much to the partygoers' discredit, however, "sometimes they came and went without having met Gatsby at all." In stark contrast, Nick "as soon as [he] arrived . . . made an attempt to find [his] host." He had little luck, however, because no one could help him. In fact, when Nick asks people for help in finding Gatsby, they can only look at him "in such an amazed way" and vehemently deny "any knowledge of his movements," again setting a stark contrast between himself and the people he tells us about.

Character Insight

The only person Nick encounters at the party whom he knows is Jordan Baker. The mere fact that Jordan is at the party suggests that she is, in some ways (ways that are explored later in this chapter and beyond) an extension of the party-going set. Although little is known of her, up to this point, her presence at the mansion suggests that she likely runs with the sort of people who frequent Gatsby's house. She seems intrigued by Nick, however, just as he is intrigued by her, for reasons that remain unstated. Perhaps she finds Nick a welcome relief to the kinds of men she generally meets, or perhaps she is drawn to his Midwestern sensibility, for it is clear he doesn't yet blend in with the East Coast crowd. Whatever it is that draws her to him, she has never before been involved with anyone quite like Nick (this is especially brought out in Chapters 8 and 9).

While Nick and Jordan mingle at Gatsby's party, they learn many intriguing things about their host, and everything they learn underscores the idea of reality versus rumor that underlies so much of *The Great Gatsby*. One of the first things the couple find out is that when one partygoer tore a dress at a party, Gatsby sent her a new evening gown worth a small fortune. Nick and Jordan also discover that part of the Gatsby mythos is that "he killed a man once." Another romantic rumor places Gatsby as "a German spy during the war." How interesting that no one really knows much about Gatsby! In a way, it is a sad commentary on the people attending the party: Can they really care so little about their host that they don't even have the common courtesy to find the difference between fiction and fact? Instead, they believe what is convenient or easy for them, creating a version of Jay Gatsby that meets their ideals. Ironically, the guests' construction of their host is not unlike how the host himself, as is later revealed, has constructed himself.

As Nick and Jordan saunter around, they also shed more light on the partygoers themselves. For example, while Nick and Jordan explore the house (under the pretense, at least, of looking for Gatsby), they meet a man know throughout the book as "Owl Eyes" due to his glasses. Two things are striking about him. First, he seems impressed that the books in Gatsby's library are real. Although this may seem merely a careless remark, in fact, it speaks volumes. Gatsby, unlike Tom, is "new money," and Owl Eyes knows it. Clearly he has spent a great deal of time among the *nouveaux riches* and knows them well enough to know that they are, by and large, about appearances. He is surprised that the books are real, expecting, instead, for them to "be a nice durable cardboard," giving the illusion of a library where none really exists. Instead, Gatsby does indeed have real books. Everything in the house, Gatsby reveals later, has been painstakingly chosen to create an image of affluence. The second revealing statement Owl Eyes makes is that he's "been drunk for about a week now." In this respect, he is a perfect poster boy for the Jazz Age, drunk to incapacitation for weeks on end.

Theme

The carnivalesque atmosphere of Gatsby's party continues as the couple heads outdoors, still searching for their host. Nick offers a telling commentary on the way of life he's witnessing, stating that after he had enough champagne, "the scene had changed before [his] eyes into something significant, elemental, and profound." Sober, this scene has no more significance than any other, but through the haze of alcohol, it seems to become steeped in meaning. Again, Fitzgerald offers candid commentary into life in the Jazz Age. He is, in effect, offering harsh social criticism, by suggesting that the only way in which a sense of meaning is to be found in this time is through altering one's sense of consciousness. Through the partying, people were able to bring meaning (regardless of the fact it may be false meaning) into their otherwise meaningless lives. For them, drinking was an escape, allowing them to exit the mundane world and take part in something bigger, something more meaningful.

The first glimpse of Gatsby reveals a man who stands apart from the type of guests he routinely hosts at his parties. Much to Fitzgerald's credit, the reader, just like Nick, falls into the trap of interacting with Gatsby before his identity is ever revealed. Nick strikes up a conversation with someone of a bit more substance than the typical party guest—someone who asks him questions about himself and is somewhat interested in him (albeit a general passing interest). In fact, as Nick remarks that Gatsby possesses "a quality of eternal reassurance . . . that you may come across four or five times in life." His smile, Nick asserts, "believed in you as you would like to believe in yourself, and assured you that it had precisely the impression of you that, at your best, you hoped to convey." The understanding projected through Gatsby's smile is not without its roots—the incidents in his past (especially those discussed in Chapter 6) have lead him to value a well-crafted appearance.

Literary Device

The image of Gatsby is one of extreme propriety. From the "majestic hand" that signed Nick's invitation to the full-sized orchestra and exquisite catering, Gatsby appears the perfect gentleman. He is gracious and kindhearted (or else how could he put up with his own guests?), a combination that gives rise to rumors. He is, however, set apart from the guests, both mentally and physically. Nick indicates that during the course of the evening, as men and women began to move closer to each other in gestures of flirtation, Gatsby was strikingly marginalized. No one sought to rest her head on his shoulder, no friends sought him out to join their small and intimate groups. Gatsby, the host, remained strikingly aloof from his guests. Nick, likely, is one of the first people to ever realize this. (Again, as a testament to his general nature, Nick comes off as a credible and trustworthy narrator.) Just as one may think that Gatsby will have nothing to do with any woman, however, he sends for Jordan Baker, wishing to speak to her privately. When Jordan returns, Fitzgerald, wanting to maintain suspense for a bit longer, withholds the purpose of their discussion, but Jordan says that it was "the most amazing thing," which is finally discussed at the end of Chapter 4.

Theme

In addition to providing information about Gatsby, his parties, and his party guests, Chapter 3 also chronicles a return to the issues of morality and equity introduced in Chapter 1. Toward the chapter's end, Nick shifts his focus away from Gatsby and toward Jordan. He reveals his interest in her, but tempers it by discussing her apparent penchant for lying. While he is initially "flattered to go places with her," largely because of her fame, he isn't "actually in love" but feels "a sort of tender curiosity." Nick's opinion of Jordan changes, however, when he finds that she makes a habit of lying her way out of bad situations, thus revealing two contrary facets of his nature. Unlike many of the novel's characters who delight in basking in the fame and notoriety of others (take for instance Myrtle's delight at the power and prestige she gets from being with Tom), Nick's judgment is not entirely clouded by fame. Even though Nick is fond of Jordan he is still able to discern her lack of honesty. However, as admirable as that is, Nick contradicts this good judgment when he confesses that "Dishonesty in a woman is a thing you never blame deeply—I was casually sorry, and then I forgot." Clearly, although he wouldn't admit it, he *does* hold a double standard, excusing Jordan's shortcomings because of her gender. As the chapter ends, Nick reveals his own sense of self worth: Of all the people he has known, he is one of the few who is honest. In many respects, this is true, and as the story continues, Nick's moral fortitude becomes more and more pronounced, but the mere fact that he has dismissed Jordan's dishonesty makes the reader wonder, at least momentarily, whether this is true.

Glossary

omnibus a bus; having a variety of purposes or uses.

fortnight a period of two weeks.

prodigality wastefulness or extreme lavishness.

The Follies immensely popular revue started by Florenz Ziegfeld in 1907.

white flannels white trousers made of light flannel.

Stoddard lectures travel books taking in the entire world.

Belasco David Belasco (1853-1931); U.S. theatrical producer, playwright, and actor.

coupe a closed, two-door automobile with a body smaller than that of a sedan.

Yale Club private social club in New York City.

Chapter 4

Summary

Chapter 4 opens with a cataloguing of Gatsby's party guests: the Chester Beckers, the Leeches, Doctor Webster Civet, the Hornbeams, the Ismays, the Chrysties, and so on. From socialites and debutantes to the famous and the infamous, Gatsby's parties draw only the most fashionable of people. One fellow, Klipspringer, in fact, was at Gatsby's house so often and so long that he became known as simply "the boarder."

One late July morning, Gatsby arrives at Nick's and announces they are having lunch that day in New York. During the "disconcerting ride" to the city, Gatsby attempts to clear the record about his past so that Nick wouldn't "get a wrong idea" by listening to the rumors. Nick is suspicious, however, when he hears Gatsby reveal that he was born into a wealthy Midwest family (in San Francisco) and educated at Oxford, "a family tradition." After touring Europe, Gatsby served as a major in the military where he "tried very hard to die" but, in his own words, "seemed to bear an enchanted life." As in testament to this disclosure, Gatsby is pulled over for speeding, but is let go after producing a card from the police commissioner for whom Gatsby had once done a favor.

In New York, two important things happen to Nick. First, at lunch Nick meets Meyer Wolfsheim, a professional gambler and the man rumored to have fixed the 1919 World Series. Wolfsheim is Gatsby's link to organized crime and there is an intimation that Gatsby may be able to fix Nick up with Wolfsheim in an undisclosed venture (this hint is again brought out in Chapter 5). The second memorable thing which happened to Nick comes through Jordan Baker. She recounts how one morning in 1917 she met Daisy and an unknown admirer, a military officer, who watched Daisy "in a way that every young girl wants to be looked at." His name: Jay Gatsby. Daisy's family didn't approve of the match and so she eventually turned her attentions away from Gatsby and to Tom Buchannan. On the day before the wedding, Daisy reconsidered her actions but after a drunken cry, she thought better of her situation and married Tom. The following April, Daisy gave birth to a daughter. Jordan continues, noting what Gatsby told her on the night of the party. Apparently, it was not coincidence that brought him to West Egg: He purposely selected his house so that the house of his lost love would be just across the bay. Jordan then relays Gatsby's request: that Nick invite Daisy over some afternoon so he can arrange to come by and see her, as if by accident. She is to know nothing about the intended reunion with her former lover; it is all supposed to be a surprise.

Commentary

All three of the major incidents in this chapter—Gatsby's disclosure in the car, the meeting with Wolfsheim, and Jordan's story about Daisy's soldier—serve one common purpose: they all give a better understanding of Jay Gatsby's past and, in turn, his present. Gatsby, as if aware of the rumors flying about him, attempts to set the record straight, but doesn't touch on every aspect of his past, only what he wishes Nick to know. Later chapters will give more and more information, even after his death.

Literary Device

The opening paragraphs of the chapter read much like a *Who's Who* of 1922. Nick expands upon an idea brought out in the prior chapter: Gatsby's party guests. Nick recounts dozens and dozens of names, all of them supposedly recognizable. Clearly, everyone who was anyone wanted to be seen at Gatsby's lavish gatherings. Some of the people came from East Egg (they are distinguished by their aristocratic-sounding names: the Endives, the Stonewall Jacksons, the Fishguards, and the Ripley Snells), while others came from West Egg (sporting more ethnic-sounding names such as Pole, Mulready, Schoen, Gulick, Cohen, Schwartze, and McCarty). Fitzgerald's use of names here brings out the notion that East Egg is symbolic of the established social order (the old money) while West Egg is home to the newcomers, people who may have equal wealth, but haven't had it nearly as long. It is curious that Nick recounts the names off notes he took on a timetable dated July 5, 1922, the day *after* Independence day, as if to indicate these people have somehow only just arrived and are enjoying the benefits of independence that they didn't even fight for.

After the conspicuous cataloguing of Gatsby's guests, Nick recounts another of his adventures—this time one that changes the course of his life forever. Gatsby, arriving at Nick's house for the first time, informs him that because they will be having lunch together, they may as well ride together. The real reason for Gatsby's visit, however, is to talk to

Nick alone, and so the two men head to the city driving Gatsby's car—so big and excessive as to border on being gaudy. (How ironic it is that a car, a massive symbol of the American dream and here an outward manifestation of Gatsby's wealth, will ultimately lead to his undoing.)

Character Insight

When the two men leave for town Nick, by his own disclosure, has little real knowledge of Gatsby, having "talked with him perhaps half a dozen times in the past month." All that soon changes, however, as Gatsby unfolds his story. The discussion is particularly important because it gives the first strong indication that Gatsby isn't quite what he presents himself to be. Up to now, there has been mystery and speculation, but Fitzgerald hasn't revealed enough of Gatsby to allow readers to figure him out. Gatsby tells Nick, "God's truth," that he comes from wealthy people in the Middle West and was "educated at Oxford." Gatsby's inability to deliver that phrase without difficulty alerts Nick that something may be amiss. When Nick questions him as to where in the Middle West he hails from, readers get their first clear indication that Gatsby is recounting an elaborate lie—"San Francisco" is hardly the Middle West, and Nick knows it. Sadly, Gatsby isn't even a good liar and he continues to tell his story, as if telling it will make it so. Fitzgerald later reveals that nearly everything (perhaps everything) he tells Nick during this ride, the candid self-disclosures he freely offers so that Nick doesn't get "a wrong idea" of him from the stories floating around, are themselves fictions created by Gatsby as part of his plan to reinvent himself. In fact, the past that Gatsby describes reads like an adventure tale, a romance in which the hero "lived like a young rajah," looking for treasures, dabbling in everything from the fine arts to big game hunting. Gatsby's past is highly unbelievable—a point not lost on Nick. When Gatsby informs Nick that his "family all died and [he] came into a good deal of money," it is wishful thinking at best, and Chapters 7 and 9 disclose that Gatsby's money came from a very different place.

As the two men head to the city, they pass through the valley of ashes, moving from a desolate gray world of dead-end dreams to the city, the place where anything at all can happen. When Gatsby is stopped for speeding, Gatsby need merely to wave a card before the officer and he is let go with a polite "Know you next time, Mr. Gatsby. Excuse *me*!" Apparently Gatsby once did a favor for the commissioner and receives his eternal thanks. Although Gatsby has just fed Nick an elaborate series of lies, this is the first piece that may well be true.

Gatsby, through a business associate whom they are on their way to see, may likely have done a favor for the commissioner—and it is likely to have been something of a questionable nature.

The luncheon with Gatsby is not remarkable, save for the character who is introduced: Meyer Wolfsheim, a notorious gambler who is rumored to have rigged the 1919 World Series, an unprecedented scandal that degraded America's Game. Mr. Wolfsheim, a business associate of Jay Gatsby, is everything his name suggests: He is a perfect combination of human and animal. He is wolf-like in his ways, and no where do we get better evidence of this than by the human molar cufflinks he sports proudly. Although Nick has begun to like Gatsby and wants to give him the benefit of the doubt, Gatsby's taste in business connections is not at all what a man who comes from the background Gatsby has just recounted would make. Wolfsheim is Gatsby's connection (or *gonnection*, as Wolfsheim would say) to the world of organized crime. Wolfsheim, as is later made known, has been instrumental in Gatsby's ability to accumulate wealth. Theirs is a partnership in which Gatsby feels some sort of indebtedness to Wolfsheim—although they are partners on some levels, they are not at all equals.

That same afternoon, after hearing Gatsby's story and meeting his business contact, Nick has tea with Jordan Baker wherein he gets a more accurate reading of Gatsby. Jordan recounts the "amazing" story she learned the night of Gatsby's party. The story recalls Jordan's girlhood in Louisville and one of her memories of Daisy Fay (who would later become Daisy Buchanan; notice, too, "Fay" is a synonym for "faerie"— an appropriate name for someone of Daisy's ethereal nature). On one memorable day, she saw Daisy with a young officer, Jay Gatsby, who looked at Daisy "in a way that every young girl wants to be looked at." The memory stayed with Jordan "because it seemed romantic." However, she didn't put the Jay Gatsby in Daisy's car with the Jay Gatsby of West Egg until the night of the party.

Through Jordan's story of Daisy right before her wedding, Fitzgerald gives a much better sense of Daisy. She loved the young officer (as Gatsby tells in Chapter 8), but was forcibly discouraged from entering into a permanent relationship with the young man—Gatsby's lack of money was his primary character deficit. After breaking off contact with Gatsby, Daisy began to resume her activities as usual. She meets Tom Buchannan and shortly becomes engaged to him. One the eve of her wedding Daisy has second thoughts, deciding while in a drunken stupor that perhaps marrying for love instead of money is what she should do. As she sobers up she seems to come to terms with herself and what is expected of her. She puts Gatsby behind her and marries Tom. Before long, however, Tom begins to have affairs. Daisy is aware of this from early on, but fails to do anything about it. One can only speculate why. Clearly Daisy is more dimensional than the initial impression of her suggests. She is aware of Tom's indiscretions, but appears not to care. Why? It's difficult to say with certainty, but one theory holds that she enjoys Tom's money and the status she has as a Buchannan of East Egg. Challenging her husband's tomcat-like behavior would jeopardize her status and security—the things her entire life has revolved around.

When Jordan finishes telling this story of Daisy, she comes to where Gatsby figures in, and Nick learns a great deal about him through this disclosure. Jordan reveals that it wasn't coincidence that Gatsby's house is across the Sound from Daisy's, as Nick initially believes. Rather, it is all part of Gatsby's calculated plan. He purposely chose the less fashionable West Egg so that he could be across from Daisy, rather than adjacent to her. Jordan also discloses that the parties he hosts are for no other reason than to try to get Daisy's attention. Gatsby, following his dream of being reunited with Daisy, puts on excessive displays of wealth, entertaining people he doesn't know and who don't know him, all for the sake of a lost love. He throws the parties initially in the hope Daisy might attend. Later, he begins to ask his guests if they know her. When he finds that Jordan is a friend of Daisy's, he tells her portions of his story. When Jordan suggests a meeting in New York, Gatsby won't hear of it. "I want to see her right next door," Gatsby protests, with the intimation that he doesn't want to trouble Daisy or Jordan or have them go out of their way. What he really wants is to have Daisy see his house, his nearly ostentatious display of money. In his mind, if Daisy knows how much he is worth, she will have no reason to reject him a second time. As the conversation ends, Jordan brings up Gatsby's request: that Nick invite Daisy over for tea so Gatsby can happen by.

Theme

The chapter's end raises some interesting questions and complications, again harkening back to the idea of morality that permeates the book. Jordan, confiding in Nick, tells him "Daisy ought to have something in her life," and Nick, by implicitly agreeing to pander for Gatsby, is in accord. Nick is placing himself in a position in which he will have to come to terms with helping deceive Tom while bringing Gatsby's fantasy to life. Nick, too, is becoming more and more involved with Jordan and this, perhaps, clouds his judgment. (At the end of Chapter 3, he was determined to break off relations with a girl back home so that he could pursue Jordan, again showing his moral nature.) As Chapter 4 ends, Nick comes to the realization that both Tom and Gatsby are linked by their pursuit of their respective dreams. Each of the men, Nick realizes, are motivated by their desire to be loved by a "disembodied face float[ing] along the dark cornices." Nick, feeling empty at the realization he has no such dream, pulls Jordan closer to him, ending the chapter with a kiss.

If nothing else, this moment of desire makes Nick seem more human. He has needs and longings, just as everyone does. In addition, his agreeing to help Gatsby reunite with Daisy suggests he, too, has a bit of the romantic about him. His morality isn't as rigid as may have been initially supposed; these small acts of human nature help warm the reader to an otherwise aloof man. This release of passion, too, marks a turning point for Nick. From this time, he is open to change and susceptible to the feeling and emotions that many other characters (especially Tom, and to a large extent Daisy and Jordan) work diligently to keep out.

Glossary

Argonne Forest a wooded region in northeast France, near the Belgian border.

1919 World Series notorious championship baseball series plagued by scandal for being fixed.

Sauterne a sweet white wine produced in southwest France near the Bordeaux region.

victoria an early touring automobile with a folding top over the rear seat.

Chapter 5

Summary

When Nick returns home to West Egg that evening, he finds Gatsby's house lit top to bottom with no party in sight, and Gatsby walking over to see him. Nick assures Gatsby that he will phone Daisy the next day and invite her to tea. Gatsby, knowing Nick doesn't make much money, offers to arrange for him to "pick up a nice bit of money." Nick, however, declines.

The next day, Nick phones Daisy and extends his invitation with the stipulation "Don't bring Tom." She accepts his invitation, agreeing on a day. The agreed upon day arrives and Gatsby, wanting everything to be perfect, sends a man to cut Nick's grass and, later, has flowers delivered. Arriving an hour before Daisy, Gatsby is nervous and, for the first time in the novel, a little unsure of himself. At the appointed time, Daisy arrives. Nick ushers Daisy into the house to find that Gatsby has disappeared, only to reemerge at the front door, looking pale and tragic. Gatsby ushers himself into the living room and joins Daisy. The reunion is initially stilted and unnaturally polite, leaving all three people feeling somewhat awkward, but amid the tea preparations, a greater sense of ease overtakes the group. Excusing himself, Nick tries to give Gatsby and Daisy some privacy, but Gatsby, as nervous as a young man, follows him out. Nick sends Gatsby back in to Daisy, while he himself sneaks out the back and wanders around the house for half an hour.

Upon his return, Nick finds Gatsby changed entirely. He has moved from the embarrassment of his initial appearance to unbounded delight, radiating a newfound sense of well-being. Daisy, too, reflects an "unexpected joy" though her voice. At Gatsby's request, the three move from Nick's little house to Gatsby's mansion. Daisy, just as Gatsby had intended, is delighted by the magnificence of his estate. Together they wander from room to room, each one tastefully and carefully decorated to create a particular ambiance. Along the way they meet Klipspringer, "the boarder," who was busy doing exercises as if he hadn't a care in the world. At the house, Gatsby passes into yet a third phase: wonder at Daisy's presence in his house. Daisy, at seeing Gatsby's array of shirts, buries her head in them weeping at their beauty. By the end of the afternoon, Gatsby has shown Daisy all the material stability he possesses, yet Nick hints that perhaps Daisy doesn't measure up—not because of a shortcoming on her part, but because of the magnitude of the dream that Gatsby has built over the past five years. At chapter's end, Nick departs, leaving Gatsby and Daisy alone together.

Commentary

Chapter 5 introduces the heart of the matter: Gatsby's dream of Daisy. Through Nick, Gatsby is brought face-to-face with the fulfillment of a dream that he has pursued relentlessly for the past five years of his life. Everything he has done has been, in some sense, tied to his pursuit of Daisy. In a sense, Daisy's and Gatsby's encounter marks the book's high point—the dream is realized. What happens after a dream is fulfilled? Unlike other novels in which characters work to overcome adversity only to have their dreams realized at the end of the book and live happily ever after (or so the implication goes), Gatsby has his dream fulfilled early, suggesting to astute readers that this won't be the typical rags-to-riches story. The second half of the book describes what happens when one chases, then obtains, one's dream. The end need not be "happily ever after."

The chapter opens as Nick returns home, only to find Gatsby's house "lit from tower to cellar," with no party in sight, only Gatsby "glancing into some of the rooms." In an attempt to calm Gatsby's apparent restlessness, Nick tells him he will phone Daisy and invite her to tea. Gatsby, still trying to play it cool, casually remarks "Oh, that's all right." Nick, who now knows a great deal more about how Gatsby functions (and the fact he has spent the last five years of his life chasing a dream), insists on pinning Gatsby down to a date. Gatsby, trying to show his appreciation, suggest he line Nick up with some of his business contacts in order to "pick up a nice bit of money" on the side. Of course, Gatsby is referring to his underworld connections, but what is perhaps so striking about Gatsby's gesture is the apparent tactlessness of it all. Despite his great wealth, his generosity takes curious and non-traditional forms showing just how far out of touch he really is with the "old money" world into which he wishes entrée.

Character Insight

On the day of the appointed visit, Gatsby arrives an hour in advance, giving us our first glimpse of his vulnerability. Wanting to make sure every detail of his meeting is perfect (meaning it measures up to his dream) Gatsby has Nick's grass cut and has "a greenhouse" of flowers delivered prior to Daisy's arrival. Gatsby dresses for the event in a "white flannel suit, silver shirt, a gold-colored tie." His clothes, like his parties, his house, and his car, are an overt reminder of his newly earned wealth. It is as if he wants to make sure Daisy does not miss the fact that he now has that one thing that eluded him before: money.

When Gatsby arrives, for the first time he shows his vulnerability and uncertainty. Up to this point, he has been collected in every situation, but when facing the biggest challenge he's faced in years, his sulking, self-conscious behavior is nearly embarrassing—the generally graceful man stammers in fright, not unlike a young boy. For the first time, Jay Gatsby seems unsure of himself.

Literary Device

At one point, in his nervousness, he knocks a broken clock off the mantel, catching it just before it hits the ground. The symbolic nature of this act cannot be overlooked. Although on one level it is just another awkward incident caused by Gatsby's nervousness, it goes beyond that. The fact the clock is stopped is significant. In a sense, the clock stopped at a specific point in time, trapped there forever, just as Gatsby's life, in many regards, stopped when he was hit with the realization that while he was poor, he could never have Daisy. Gatsby is, in essence, trapped by his dreams of ideal love with Daisy, just as the clock is trapped in that exact moment when it stopped working. Following this analysis through to its final conclusion, one must wonder if Fitzgerald isn't also trying to say that Gatsby's dream stopped his growth in some respects (specifically emotionally); he's been so busy chasing a dream rather than enjoying reality, that like the clock, he is frozen in time.

As the afternoon unfolds, Jay and Daisy grow more comfortable in each other's presence. After excusing himself, allowing Daisy and Gatsby the opportunity to be alone together, Nick returns to find Gatsby glowing; "without a word or gesture of exultation a new well-being radiated from him and filled the little room." Daisy, too, appears equally moved by the meeting and (not surprisingly) her voice, "full of aching, grieving beauty" gives away her happiness at the meeting. When Gatsby nears the peak of his comfort, he suggests the party adjourn to his house.

As the three people make their way up to and through Gatsby's mansion, Gatsby revels in the impact his belongings have on Daisy. They have, in essence, accomplished that which he intended: They impress her. In fact, Gatsby is able to "[revalue] everything in his house according to the measure of response it drew from her well-love eyes." Keep this image in mind during Chapter 9, when it is inverted as Gatsby's father revalues his son based on the beauty and number of his material possessions. In another of the book's memorable images, Gatsby takes out a pile of shirts and throws them in the air. The shirts keep coming, and Gatsby keeps throwing them. Shirts of every color, every style, and every texture become strewn about the room in a glaringly obvious display of his wealth. How can a man who isn't well off afford to have such an array of shirts? The shirt's impact is not lost on Daisy, who is always appreciative of a great display of materialism. In fact, the excess and bounty of Gatsby's shirts causes her to put her face into them and cry, sad because she's "never seen such—such beautiful shirts before." Although a seemingly non-sensical statement, it is really a good indication of her true nature. She isn't weeping for a lost love; rather she is weeping at the overt display of wealth she sees before her.

When the trio attempts to move down to the waterfront they are held up by the rain, giving Gatsby the opportunity to make a telling statement. He informs Daisy, who clearly has no idea, that her house is right across the Sound from where they are standing. He then continues, informing her "You always have a green light that burns all night at the end of your dock." Gatsby's admission of this secret is lost neither on Nick nor on Gatsby himself (according to Nick). Daisy, however, remains oblivious to its meaning. She is unable to grasp that by Gatsby telling her this, he has shared one of his most sanctified rituals. Prior to that day, the green light (representing many things: hope, youth, forward momentum, money) represented a dream to him and by reaching out to it, he was bringing himself closer to his love. Now that she was standing beside him, her arm in his, the light will no longer hold the same significance. His dream, the goal for which he patterned most of his adult life on, must now change.

Gatsby and Daisy are, as is evidenced in this chapter, generally a good match. Gatsby's dreamlike nature compliments nicely Daisy's ethereal qualities. Gatsby, the collector of "enchanted objects," as Nick says, seems the perfect match for the otherworldly Daisy who runs exclusively on emotional responses. As if caught up in Gatsby's dream vision, Daisy calls him to the window to look at the "pink and golden billow of foamy clouds," declaring to Gatsby that she'd "like to just get one of those pink clouds and put you in it and push you around."

As the chapter ends, Nick, the trusted voice of reason, offers an astute reading on the whole situation. He interprets a look of Gatsby's face to indicate that perhaps he is dissatisfied with the whole affair. What occurs to Nick, and perhaps to Gatsby, is that once a dream is achieved, life must still continue. How does one go about the business of reordering his life after bringing a fabrication, a fantasy, to life? For Gatsby, who has spent the past five years dreaming of Daisy, one wonders whether through the five years he was in love with Daisy, or the *idea* of Daisy. His relentless pursuit of his dream has allowed him ample opportunity to construct scenarios in his head and to imagine her not necessarily as she is, but as he perceives her to be. As Gatsby peers into Daisy's eyes and listens to her enchanting voice, he becomes more and more in love with the vision he has conjured in front of him. As the chapter closes, Daisy and Gatsby have become so lost in each other that Nick ceases to exist for them. In response, Nick quietly retreats, leaving the lovers alone together.

Glossary

Kant Immanuel Kant (1724–1804); German philosopher.

Chapter 6

Summary

Chapter 6 opens with an air of suspicion as a reporter comes to Gatsby, asking him "if he had anything to say." The myth of Gatsby was becoming so great by summer's end that he was rumored to be embroiled in a variety of plots and schemes, inventions that provided a source of satisfaction to Gatsby, who was originally christened James Gatz and hails from North Dakota. Nick fills the reader in on Gatsby's real background, which is in sharp contrast to the fabricated antecedents Gatsby told Nick during their drive to New York. James Gatz became Jay Gatsby on the fateful day when, on the shores of Lake Superior, he saw Dan Cody drop anchor on his yacht. Prior to that time, Gatsby spent part of his young adulthood roaming parts of Minnesota shaping the aspects of the persona he would assume. Nick suspects he had the name ready prior to meeting Cody, but it was Cody who gave Gatsby the opportunity to hone the fiction that would define his life. Cody, fifty years old with a penchant for women, took Gatsby under his wing and prepared him for the yachting life, and they embarked for the West Indies and the Barbary Coast. During their five years together, Cody and Gatsby went around the continent three times; in the end, Cody was mysteriously undone by his lady love.

After many weeks of not seeing Gatsby (largely because Nick was too busy spending time with Jordan), Nick goes to visit. Shortly after his arrival, Tom Buchannan and two others out for a horseback ride show up for a drink. After exchanging social small talk wherein Gatsby is invited to dine with the group, the three riders abruptly leave without him, somewhat taken aback that he accepted what they deem to be a purely rhetorical invitation.

Tom, apparently concerned with Daisy's recent activities, accompanies her to one of Gatsby's parties. Gatsby tries to impress the Buchanans by pointing out all the celebrities present, then makes a point of introducing Tom, much to his unease, as "the polo player." Gatsby and Daisy dance, marking the only time Gatsby really gets involved with one of his own parties. Later, Daisy and Gatsby adjourn to Nick's steps for a half-hour of privacy. They head back to the party and when dinner arrives, Tom remarks he wishes to eat with another group. Daisy, always aware of what Tom is really up to, remarks the girl is "common but pretty" and offers a pencil in case he wants to take down an address. Daisy, aside from the half-hour she spends with Gatsby, finds the party unnerving and appalling. After the Buchanans leave and the party breaks up, Nick and Gatsby review the evening. Gatsby, fearing Daisy did not have a good time, worries about her. When Nick cautions Gatsby that "You can't repeat the past," Gatsby idealistically answers "Why of course you can!" words that strike Nick soundly because of their "appalling sentimentality," which both delights and disgusts him.

Commentary

Literary Device

If Chapter 5 showed Gatsby achieving his dream, Chapter 6 demonstrates just how deeply his dream runs. Much of the mystery surrounding Gatsby is cleared away in this chapter and the reader learns more about who he really is, where he comes from, and what he believes. After seeing Gatsby and getting to know him, Nick presents the real story of his past. By holding the actual story until Chapter 6, Fitzgerald accomplishes two things: First and most obviously, he builds suspense and piques the reader's curiosity. Second, and of equal importance, Fitzgerald is able to undercut the image of Gatsby. Ever so subtly, Fitzgerald presents, in effect, an exposé. Much as Nick did, one feels led on—Gatsby is not at all the man he claims to be. Fitzgerald wants the readers to feel delighted, glad for someone to succeed by his own ingenuity, we also a little unnerved at the ease in which Gatsby has been able to pull off his charade.

The chapter opens with an increased flurry of suspicion surrounding Gatsby. Much to his delight, the rumors about him are flying as furiously as ever, even bringing a wayward reporter to investigate (although what, precisely, he was investigating he wouldn't say). Rumors about Gatsby's past abound by the end of the summer, making a perfect segue for Nick to tell the real story on his neighbor—James Gatz from North Dakota. Gatsby is, in reality, a creation, a fiction brought to life. He is the fabrication of a young Midwestern dreamer, the son of "shiftless and unsuccessful farm people" who spent his youth planning how he would escape the monotony of his everyday life—a life he never really accepted at all. He craved adventures and the embodiment of the romantic ideal, and so he voluntarily left his family to make his own way. In many senses, Gatsby's story is the rags-to-riches American dream. A young man from the middle of nowhere, through his own ingenuity and resourcefulness, makes it big.

But there is a decided downside to this American dream. For Gatsby, his life began at age seventeen when he met Dan Cody. In the years since, he has traveled the globe, gaining, losing, and regaining his fortune. All of his money, however, doesn't exactly place him within the social strata to which he aspires. His wealth may allow him to enter certain social circles otherwise forbidden, but he is unprepared to function fully in them (just as in Chapter 5 when Gatsby tries to thank Nick for his kindness by offering to bring him into a suspicious, yet lucrative, business arrangement). Although money is a large part of the American dream, through Gatsby one sees that just having money isn't enough. In this chapter in particular, Fitzgerald clearly points out the distinction between "new money" and "old money" and, regardless of the amount of wealth one accumulates, where the money comes from and how long it's been around matters just as much as how much of it there is.

Character Insight

Another downside to Gatsby's American dream is that it has, in essence, stunted his growth, intellectually, spiritually, and emotionally. As noted, James ("Jimmy") Gatz ceased to exist on the day Gatsby was born, the day he rowed out in Lake Superior to meet Dan Cody (whose name alone is meant to evoke images of Daniel Boone and "Buffalo Bill" Cody, two oftentimes romanticized frontier figures). Since that time, he has worked to flesh out a fully dimensional fiction. When the persona he created, Jay Gatsby, fell in love with Daisy Fay, his fate was, in essence, sealed. As Gatsby became fixed on winning Daisy, his whole life became ordered around that goal. And why not? After all, he had willed Jay Gatsby into existence, why couldn't he will Daisy to be with him. It is worth pointing out, too, that there is little growth on Gatsby's part from the time he is seventeen until his death. He remains inexorably tied to his dreams and blindly pursues them at all costs. In one sense, Gatsby's determination is commendable, but there comes a point where living in a fictive world is detrimental to one's self, as Gatsby will find out all too soon. Dreams and goals are good, but not when they consume the dreamer.

After filling in Gatsby's background, Nick tells of a day at Gatsby's when three riders (Tom, Mr. Sloane, and an unnamed young woman) stop in for a drink. Gatsby, ever the good host, receives them warmly, although he knows full well that Tom is Daisy's husband. Although in some sense this may seem a strange interlude lacking in development and purpose, it is, in effect, intricately tied to the story of Dan Cody and the evolution of Jay Gatsby. The riders' visit is in many ways akin to the observations Nick made in Chapter 3 when he experienced his first Gatsby party. Just as at the party Gatsby stood away from the crowd (many of whom didn't even know him), Gatsby stands alone in this smaller setting as well. The three drop by to drink his liquor and little else. Their concern for him is minimal and their purposes mercenary. Under the pretense of sociability, the young woman invites Gatsby to join them for dinner. The three riders know the invitation is rhetorical—just a formality that is not meant to be accepted. Gatsby, however, is unable to sense the invitation's hollowness and agrees to attend. The group, appalled at his behavior, sneaks out without him, marveling, at his poor taste.

This scenario contains several valuable messages. First, it gives an example of how shallow and mean-spirited "old money" can be. The trio's behavior is nothing less than appalling. Second, Gatsby takes their words at face value, trusting them to mean what they say. While this is a commendable trait, reflective of Gatsby's good nature and dreamer disposition, it leads to a third realization: that no matter how much Gatsby is living the American dream, the "old money" crowd will never accept him. Try as he might, Gatsby remains outside the inner sanctum and nothing he can do will allow him full access. He will never be accepted by anyone but the *nouveaux riches*.

The final incident of the chapter is the party at its end, the first and only party Daisy attends, and is, in many ways, unlike any party Gatsby has hosted so far. Up to this point, the purpose of the parties was twofold: to get Daisy's attention or, failing that, to make contact with someone who knows her. Now, for the first time, she's in attendance (with Tom, no less), so the party's purpose must necessarily change. Daisy and Gatsby have become increasingly comfortable with each other and even Tom is beginning to feel somewhat threatened by Daisy's "running around alone." At the party, Gatsby tries his best to impress the Buchanans by pointing out all the famous guests. Tom and Daisy, however, are remarkably unimpressed, although Tom does seem to be having a better time after he finds a woman to pursue and Daisy, not surprisingly, is drawn to the luminescent quality of the movie star (who is, in many ways, a sister to Daisy). By and large, though, Tom and especially Daisy are unimpressed by the West Eggers. The "raw vigor" of the party disgusts them, offending their "old money" sensibilities, providing another example of how the Buchanans and the people they represent discriminate on the basis of social class.

After Tom and Daisy head home, Nick and Gatsby debrief the evening's events. Gatsby, worried that Daisy didn't have a good time (after all, the Daisy in his dream would have a good time), shares his concern with Nick. Carraway, always the gentle voice of reason, reminds his friend that the past is in the past and it can't be resurrected. Most would agree with this, which makes Gatsby's "Why of course you can!" even more striking. There is no mistaking Gatsby's personality: He's like an errant knight, seeking to capture the illusive grail. He is living in the past, something the reader may not have known, had he not realized his dream of reuniting with Daisy. Although it would be going too far to say Gatsby is weak in character, Fitzgerald creates a protagonist who is unable to function in the present. He must continually return to the past, revising it and modifying it until it takes on epic qualities which, sadly, can never be realized in the everyday world. Gatsby, just as he is at his parties and with the social elite, is once again marginalized, forced to the fringes by the vivacity of his dream.

Glossary

meretricious alluring by false, showy charms; attractive in a flashy way; tawdry.

Madame de Maintenon (1635–1719); second wife of Louis XIV of France. She is often depicted as ambitious, greedy, evil, and narrow-minded.

dilatory inclined to delay; slow or late in doing things.

Chapter 7

Summary

As the curiosity surrounding Gatsby peaks, the routine Saturday parties abruptly cease. When Gatsby comes, at Daisy's request, to invite him to lunch at her house the next day, Nick learns that Gatsby replaced the servants with "some people Wolfsheim wanted to do something for"—he feared they would leak information about he and Daisy. The day, it turns out, is unbearably hot, making all the participants in the luncheon—Daisy, Gatsby, Nick, Jordan, and Tom—even more uncomfortable than expected. While all five are at the Buchanans' house, Tom leaves the room to speak with his mistress on the phone and Daisy boldly kisses Gatsby, declaring her love for him. Later, after Daisy suggests they go to town, Tom witnesses a soft glance that passes between Daisy and Gatsby and can no longer deny the two of them are having an affair.

Enraged by what he has just learned, Tom agrees they should go to the city. He retrieves a bottle of whiskey and the group starts out—Tom, Jordan, and Nick driving Gatsby's car, and Gatsby and Daisy in Tom's. Tom, it turns out, has been suspicious of Gatsby all along and has had him investigated. Noticing the car is low on gas, Tom pulls into Wilson's station where he finds Wilson visibly unwell. Wilson abruptly announces he and Myrtle will be headed West shortly because he has just learned of her secret life, although the identity of Myrtle's lover is yet unknown to him. Tom, doubly enraged at the potential loss of his mistress and his wife, malevolently questions Gatsby after the group assembles at the Plaza Hotel. He confronts Gatsby about his love for Daisy. Gatsby, refusing to be intimidated, tells Tom, "Your wife doesn't love you . . . She's never loved you. She loves me." Tom, in disbelief, turns to Daisy for confirmation. Daisy, however, cannot honestly admit she never loved Tom. Gatsby, somewhat shaken by the scene unfolding before him—the collapse of his carefully constructed dream—tries another tactic. He declares: "Daisy's leaving you." Tom assures him Daisy will never leave him for a bootlegger. Tom orders Daisy and Gatsby to head home (in Gatsby's own car this time). Tom, Jordan, and Nick follow in Tom's car.

The narration now skips to George Wilson who has been found ill by his neighbor, Michaelis. Wilson explains he has Myrtle locked inside and she will remain so until they leave in two day's time. Michaelis, astonished, heads back to his restaurant. He returns a few hours later, hears Myrtle's voice, and then sees her break away from her husband and rush into the road. As she enters the highway Myrtle is struck by a passing car that fails to stop, continuing its route out of the city. Nick, Tom, and Jordan arrive on the scene shortly. Excited by the thought of something going on, Tom pulls over to investigate. He is grief-stricken to find Myrtle's lifeless body lying on a worktable. Tom learns the car that struck Myrtle matches Gatsby's in description. Tom, visibly upset by the day's events, can only whimper of his anger toward the man he already hates.

Returning to East Egg, Tom invites Nick inside to wait for a cab to take him home. Nick, seeing clearly the moral and spiritual corruption of Tom, Daisy, and the whole society they represent, declines. Outside the Buchanans', Nick bumps into Gatsby, who asks if there was trouble on the road. Nick recounts what he has seen. After asking a few questions, Nick learns Daisy, not Gatsby, was driving at the time. Gatsby, however, in true chivalric fashion, says he'll take the blame. The chapter ends with Gatsby, the paragon of chivalry and lost dreams, remaining on vigil outside Daisy's house in case she needs assistance dealing with Tom, while Nick heads back to West Egg.

Commentary

Everything *The Great Gatsby* has been building toward intersects in this very important chapter. All of the paths, once loosely related at best, now converge—forcefully and fatally. The turbulence of Chapter 7 gives clear indications of what Gatsby, Daisy, Tom, and even Nick are about. Unfortunately, for three of the four, the revelations are complementary. As the weather of the novel becomes increasingly hotter and more oppressive, Fitzgerald finally gets to the heart of the love triangle between Gatsby, Daisy, and Tom, but lets it speak poorly of all the participants. Nick, alone, comes out of this chapter looking stronger. Like all the other characters, he has been tested in this chapter, but much to his credit, he grows and develops in a positive way.

This chapter put Gatsby and Tom side-by-side. While this happened briefly in Chapter 6, here the two men take each other on, head-to-head. Tom can no longer deny that Gatsby and Daisy are having an affair (specifics about that affair are, however, sketchy. The only item of significance is that the affair is an extension of Gatsby's dream and it leads him to the destruction of the dream and of himself). Within hours of learning of his wife's indiscretions, Tom learns that in addition to perhaps losing his wife, he is most certainly losing his mistress. This double loss enrages Tom and he strikes violently at the man he perceives as being responsible—a man who is, in his eyes, a low-class hustler, a bootlegger who will never be able to distance himself from his past. In Tom's elitist mind, Gatsby is common and therefore his existence is meaningless: He comes from ordinary roots and can never change that.

By chapter's end, Gatsby has been fully exposed. Gone are the mysterious rumors and the self-made myth. Stripped of all his illusions, he stands outside Daisy's house, vulnerable and tragically alone. Although he begins the chapter with his customary Gatsby dignity, when he comes up against Tom's hardness, the illusion of Jay Gatsby comes tumbling down. In all of Gatsby's years of dreaming, he never once suspected that he might not have his way (as is the nature of dreaming; one never dreams of having people stand in the way, preventing fantasies from coming true). As soon as Gatsby has to contend with people whose parts he can't script, he's at a loss. Instead, he will try, at all costs, to hold on to his dream. It is, in a sense, the only thing that is real to him. Without it (sadly), he is no longer able to define himself; therefore, the dream must be maintained at all costs (even when the dream has past its prime). The best example of Gatsby's last-chance efforts to save his dream come after he tries to get Daisy to admit she never loved Tom. When she admits to having actually loved Tom, Gatsby, unwilling to give up, pushes the situation forward, abruptly telling Tom "Daisy's leaving you." Tom laughs off this declaration, dismissing the whole party and ordering Daisy and Gatsby to head back in Gatsby's car. By following Tom's command, the lovers, in effect, admit defeat and Gatsby's dream disintegrates.

Character
Insight

In addition to getting the real scoop on Gatsby, one also sees the real Daisy. She has relatively few lines, but what she utters, and later what she does, changes her persona forever. Whereas in the previous chapters she has come off as shy and sweet, a little vapid, but decidedly charming, here, there is a bit more depth to her—but what lies beneath the surface isn't necessarily good. Daisy's reasons for having an affair with Gatsby aren't at all the same reasons he is in love with her. By boldly kissing Gatsby when Tom leaves the room early in Chapter 7, then declaring "You know I love you" loudly enough for all to hear (much to Jordan and Nick's discomfiture) Daisy has, in effect, shown that to her, loving Gatsby is a game whose sole purpose is to try and get back at Tom. She's playing the games on her own terms, trying to prove something to her husband (her response to Tom's rough questioning later at the hotel also supports this idea). The other early vision of Daisy is of the peacekeeper (although one wonders why she would want Tom and Gatsby both at the same outing). On the hot summer day, it is Daisy who suggests they move the party to town (largely in an attempt to keep everyone happy). Strange things, however, always happen in the city—in the land of infinite possibilities. By changing the location, the action also shifts.

As the chapter continues and the party moves to the neutral, yet magical, land of the city, the real Daisy begins to emerge, culminating in her fateful refusal to be part of Gatsby's vision. In a sense, she betrays him, leaving him to flounder helplessly against Tom's spite and anger. Finally, by the end of the chapter, the mask of innocence has come off and Daisy is exposed. Her recklessness has resulted in Myrtle's brutal death. To make matters worse, one even senses that Daisy, in fact, tried to kill Myrtle. Gatsby has a hard time admitting that the object of his love has, in fact, not merely hit and killed another person, but has fled the scene as well.

Myrtle's death by Gatsby's great car is certainly no accident. The details are sketchy, but in having Myrtle run down by Gatsby's roadster, Fitzgerald is sending a clear message. Gatsby's car, the "death car," assumes a symbolic significance as a clear and obvious manifestation of American materialism. What more obvious way to put one's wealth and means on display than through the biggest, fanciest car around. Yes, it is tragic that Myrtle dies so brutally, but her death takes on greater meaning when one realizes that it is materialism that brought about her end. Looking back to Chapter 2, it is clear that Myrtle aspires to wealth and privilege. She wants all the material comforts money can provide—and isn't at all above lording her wealth over others (such as her sister, or Nick, or the McKees). Her desire for money (which allows access to all things material) led her to have an affair with Tom (she got involved with him initially because of the fashionable way he was dressed). Myrtle's death is sadly poetic; a woman who spent her life acquiring material possessions by whatever means possible, has been, in effect, killed by her own desires. Dwelling too much on material things, Fitzgerald says, can not bring a positive resolution. Materialism can only bring misery, as seen through Myrtle.

Wilson, too, becomes more dimensional in the chapter, which is necessary in order to prepare adequately for the chapter to follow. While Wilson isn't necessarily good, he is pure. His distress at finding out about his wife's secret life is genuine but, being a man of little means and few wits, he doesn't know what to do about it. Clearly he loves Myrtle deeply—so deeply, in fact, that he would lock her in a room to prevent her running away (he plans to take her West in a few day's time, showing once again that in Fitzgerald's mind, there is something more pure, more sensible, about the West). Wilson is meant to stand opposite Tom, and the way the two men respond first to their wives infidelities, and later to Myrtle's death, show that although one man is rich and the other poor, they still have much in common. In the end, however, the poor man comes off as the more passionate and heartfelt in his grief.

Nick is the only character to make it out of this chapter in better shape than when he went in. He has, of course, remembered that it was his thirtieth birthday during this chapter (remember, Fitzgerald himself was only 29 when this book was published so it is likely he saw thirty as a milestone for his narrator, as well as himself). For Nick, the change marks a passage away from youthful idealism (even ignorance). Although Nick begins the chapter much as in prior chapters (a bit uncomfortable with the Buchannans and what they represent, but not at all willing to take a stand against them), by the end he has seen quite clearly what Daisy, Tom, and Jordan are about. After Myrtle's death, Nick is plainly shaken and as a man of moral conscience, he has look at his life and those around him. When Tom, Jordan, and Nick return home after the accident, Tom invites Nick in. This is where Nick shows what he's really made of. Rather than accept Tom's invitation, as expected, he tells the reader "I'd be damned if I'd go in; I'd had enough of all of them for one day." Gone is the fellow who walked the line between the working class and the upper class. Gone is the fellow who withheld judgment because not everyone "had the advantages that [he's] had." Finally, Nick has grown up enough to take a clear moral stand. His opinion of the Buchannans becomes clear and continues to ripen until he finally can stand it no longer and heads back to the Midwest at the end of the book (again, Fitzgerald is showing the Midwest as a Utopia).

The final image in the chapter is perhaps the most pathetic in the whole book. For some readers it will tug on their heartstrings, for others it will be a defining moment, showing the true Jay Gatsby. After Jay and Daisy return to East Egg, Gatsby waits outside her house, calling to Nick as he passes. He makes a strikingly odd figure with his pink suit glowing luminously in the moonlight. When Nick inquires as to wha he's doing, Gatsby, ever the dreamer, replies he is keeping watch, in case Daisy should need his help. Although Gatsby has assumed the guise of a knight-errant before, nowhere does he seem so clearly on a quest (and a quest doomed to failure) than right here, willing to sacrifice his own life for Daisy's. (Besides, what good is a dream that has been destroyed? What's worth living for?) What escapes Gatsby, but is perfectly clear to Nick, is that his surveillance is unnecessary; there is no chance of Daisy having trouble with Tom. Both Tom and Daisy's actions at the hotel have shown just how alike they are and in a time of crisis, there is no question they will join together. Daisy is likely unaware (or at least unconcerned) with Gatsby's feelings; Tom, while perhaps sad about Myrtle's death, likely sees her as he sees everyone who isn't of his social class—an expendable object. And so Gatsby, utterly lost now that his dream has died, holds on to the last piece of all he's ever known as an adult by standing guard at Daisy's. Unfortunately for him, it will be a long night.

Glossary

Trimalchio wealthy character who lavishly feasts guests at a banquet in Petronius' *Satyricon*, a satire on Roman life in the first century A.D.

caravansary in the Near and Middle East, a kind of inn with a large central court, where caravans stop for the night.

medium a person through whom communications are thought to be sent to the living from spirits of the dead.

Chapter 8

Summary

Nick wakes as Chapter 8 opens, hearing Gatsby return home from his all-night vigil at the Buchannans. He goes to Gatsby's, feeling he should tell him something (even he doesn't know what, exactly). Gatsby reveals that nothing happened while he kept his watch. Nick suggests Gatsby leave town for a while, certain Gatsby's car would be identified as the "death car." Nick's comments make Gatsby reveal the story of his past, "because 'Jay Gatsby' had broken up like glass against Tom's hard malice." Daisy, Gatsby reveals, was his social superior, yet they fell deeply in love. The reader also learns that, when courting, Daisy and Gatsby had been intimate with each other and it was this act of intimacy that bonded him to her inexorably, feeling "married to her." Gatsby left Daisy, heading off to war. He excelled in battle and when the war was over, he tried to get home, but ended up at Oxford instead. Daisy didn't understand why he didn't return directly and, over time, her interest began to wain until she eventually broke off their relationship.

Moving back to the present, Gatsby and Nick continue their discussion of Daisy and how Gatsby had gone to Louisville to find her upon his return to the United States. She was on her honeymoon and Gatsby was left with a "melancholy beauty," as well as the idea that if he had only searched harder he would have found her. The men are finishing breakfast as Gatsby's gardener arrives. He says he plans on draining the pool because the season is over, but Gatsby asks him to wait because he hasn't used the pool at all. Nick, purposely moving slowly, heads to his train. He doesn't want to leave Gatsby, impulsively declaring "They're a rotten crowd . . . You're worth the whole damn bunch put together."

For Nick, the day drags on; he feels uneasy, preoccupied with the past day's adventures. Jordan phones, but Nick cuts her off. He phones Gatsby and, unable to reach him, decides to head home early. The narrative again shifts time and focus, as Fitzgerald goes back in time, to the evening prior, in the valley of ashes. George Wilson, despondent at Myrtle's death, appears irrational when Michaelis attempts to engage him in conversation. By morning, Michaelis is exhausted and returns home to sleep. When he returns four hours later, Wilson is gone and has traveled to Port Roosevelt, Gads Hill, West Egg, and ultimately, Gatsby's house. There he finds Gatsby floating on an air mattress in the pool. Wilson, sure that Gatsby is responsible for his wife's death, shoots and kills Gatsby. Nick finds Gatsby's body floating in the pool and, while starting to the house with the body, the gardener discovers Wilson's lifeless body off in the grass.

Commentary

Chapter 8 displays the tragic side of the American dream as Gatsby is gunned down by George Wilson. The death is brutal, if not unexpected, and brings to an end the life of the paragon of idealism. The myth of Gatsby will continue, thanks to Nick who relays the story, but Gatsby's death loudly marks the end of an era. In many senses, Gatsby is the dreamer inside all of everyone. Although the reader cheers him as he pursues his dreams, one also knows that pure idealism cannot survive in the harsh modern world. This chapter, as well as the one following, also provides astute commentary on the world that, in effect, allowed the death of Gatsby.

Character Insight

As the story opens, Nick is struggling with the situation at hand. He grapples with what's right and what's wrong, which humanizes him and lifts him above the rigid callousness of the story's other characters. Unable to sleep (a premonition of bad things to come) he heads to Gatsby's who is returning from his all-night vigil outside Daisy's house. Nick, always a bit more levelheaded and sensitive to the world around him than the other characters, senses something large is about to happen. Although he can't put his finger on it, his moral sense pulls him to Gatsby's. Upon his arrival, Gatsby seems genuinely surprised his services were not necessary outside Daisy's house, showing again just how little he really knows her.

As the men search Gatsby's house for cigarettes, the reader leans more about both Nick and Gatsby. Nick moves further and further from the background to emerge as a forceful presence in the novel, showing genuine care and concern for Gatsby, urging him to leave the city for his own protection. Throughout the chapter, Nick is continually pulled toward his friend, anxious for reasons he can't exactly articulate. Whereas Nick shows his true mettle in a flattering light in this chapter, Gatsby doesn't fare as well. He becomes weaker and more helpless, despondent in the loss of his dream. It is as if he refuses to admit that the story hasn't turned out as he intended. He refuses to acknowledge that the illusion that buoyed him for so many years has vanished, leaving him hollow and essentially empty.

As the men search Gatsby's house for the illusive cigarettes, Gatsby fills Nick in on the real story. For the first time in the novel, Gatsby sets aside his romantic view of life and confronts the past he has been trying to run from, as well as the present he has been trying to avoid. Daisy, it turns out, captured Gatsby's love largely because "she was the first 'nice' girl he had ever known." She moved in a world Gatsby aspired to and unlike other people of that particular social set, she acknowledged Gatsby's presence in that world. Although he doesn't admit it, his love affair with Daisy started early, when he erroneously defined her not merely by who she was, but by what she had and what she represented. All through the early days of their courtship, however, Gatsby tormented himself with his unworthiness, knowing "he was in Daisy's house by a colossal accident," although he led Daisy to believe he was a man of means. Although his original intention was to use Daisy, he found out that he was incapable of doing so. When their relation became intimate, he still felt unworthy, and with the intimacy, Gatsby found himself wedded, not to Daisy directly, but to the quest to prove himself worthy of her. (How sad that Gatsby's judgment is so clouded with societal expectation that he can't see that a young, idealistic man who has passion, drive, and persistence is worth more than ten Daisys put together.)

In loving Daisy, it turns out, Gatsby was trapped. On one hand, he loved her and she loved him, or more precisely, he loved what he envisionedher to be and she loved the persona he presented to her—and therein lies the rub. Both Daisy and Gatsby were in love with projected images and while Daisy didn't realize this at first, Gatsby did, and it forced him more directly into his dream world. After the war (in which Gatsby really did excel), Gatsby could have returned home to Daisy. The only difficulty with that, however, would have been that in being with Daisy, he would run the risk of being exposed as an imposter. So, rather than risk having his dream disintegrate in front of him, he perpetuated his illusion by studying at Oxford before heading back to the States. Daisy's letters begged him to return, not understanding why he wasn't rushing back to be with her. She was missing the post-war euphoria sweeping the nation and she wanted her dashing officer by her side. Eventually Daisy moved again into society, feeling the need to have some stability and purpose in her life. However, Daisy's lack of principle shows when she is willing to use love, money, or practicality (whichever was handier) to determine the direction of her life. She wanted to be married. When Tom arrived, he seemed the obvious choice, and so Daisy sent Gatsby a letter at Oxford.

The letter, it turns out, brought Gatsby back stateside. It is as if now that Daisy was married he could return and not have to fear being found out. He could carry his love for Daisy around with him, knowing full well that she was unobtainable. Although Gatsby isn't likely to admit it, in a way, Daisy marrying Tom was the perfect solution to his situation because now that she was married to another, she need never know how poor he really was. After returning to the U.S., Gatsby travels to Louisville with his last bit of money, and there the quest begins in earnest. From this moment, he spends his days trying to recapture the beauty that he basked in while with young Daisy Fay.

Upon hearing Gatsby's true story, Nick cannot help but be moved and spends the rest of the day worrying about his friend. While in the city, Nick tries desperately to keep focused on his work, but can't seem to do so. What he has realized (through Gatsby's story and the events of the previous night), and part of what is troubling him, is that he has come to know the shallowness of "polite society." Gatsby, a dreamer from nowhere, has passion and genuinely cares about something, even if it is a dream, and that is more than can be said for people like the Buchanans and Jordan Baker. In fact, when Jordan phones Nick at work he is unwilling to speak to her, finding himself more and more irritated by her shallow and self-serving ways. In rejecting her (the first man ever to do so) Nick has grown, not only seeing what dark stuff that socialites are really made of, but possessing the courage to stand against it.

Midway through the chapter, Fitzgerald shifts focus to the valley of ashes and has Nick recount what had gone on there in the hours prior. George Wilson has become overwhelmed with grief at the loss of his wife. Directly contrasting Tom Buchanan (who is unable to experience a heartfelt emotion), George is devastated and overwhelmed by emotion. His neighbor, Michaelis, tries to console him, but nothing seems to help. George lives in an effectual wasteland, void of spirituality, void of life, and when in his grief he tells Michaelis of his last day with Myrtle, he turns to the giant billboard above him. In what is perhaps his most lucid statement in the whole book, Wilson explains the purpose of Doctor T. J. Eckleburg's enormous eyes. They are the eyes of God, and "God sees everything."

Wilson's grief knows no bounds and while Michaelis sleeps, he heads in to town, eventually tracking Gatsby down and killing him while he floats on an air mattress in his swimming pool. Fitzgerald has made clear earlier in the chapter that autumn is at hand, and it naturally brings with it the ending of life—natural and human, both. Wilson, still overcome by grief and the bad judgment it invokes, finds his way to Gatsby's house (tipped off by Tom, as Nick discovers in Chapter 9) and kills Gatsby, mistakenly thinking that he is responsible for Myrtle's death.

Gatsby's death, alone in his pool, brings forth a couple of distinct images. On the one hand, his death is a rebirth of sorts. Gatsby has done nothing more than follow a dream, and despite his money and his questionable business dealings, he is nothing at all like the East Egg socialites he runs with. One admires him, if for no other reason than his ability to sustain a dream in a world that is historically inhospitable to dreamers. His death has, in a sense, removed him from his mortal existence and allowed him rebirth into a different, hopefully better, life. As Nick says, Gatsby "must have felt that he had lost the old warm world" when his dream died, and found no reason to go on. In that sense, Wilson's murdering him is a welcome end. On another level, Gatsby's death at the hands of George Wilson makes his quest complete. His dream is completely dead, but he can make one more chivalric gesture: He can be killed in Daisy's stead. By lying in the pool, Gatsby is doing nothing to protect himself, as if he saying that he won't refuse whatever is ahead of him. In some sense, Gatsby helps Wilson by refusing to be proactive in his own defense. Until the very end, Gatsby remains the dreamer, that most rare of jewels in the modern world.

Glossary

pneumatic filled with compressed air.

Chapter 9

Summary

The book's final chapter begins with the police and the paparazzi storming Gatsby's house. Nick becomes worried that he is handling Gatsby's burial arrangements, believing there must be someone closer to Gatsby who should be conducting the business at hand. When he phones Daisy to tell her of Gatsby's death, he learns she and Tom have left on a trip, leaving no itinerary. Nick, with increasing frustration, feels he must "get somebody" for Gatsby. In his mind, Gatsby did not deserve to be alone. Hoping to gather Gatsby's friends, Nick sends for Meyer Wolfsheim the next day. Wolfsheim, much to Nick's dismay, sends a letter explaining he won't be involved with Gatsby's funeral. Later that afternoon when Gatsby's phone rings, Nick answers. Upon telling the speaker that Gatsby is dead, the speaker hangs up.

Three days after Gatsby dies, Nick receives a telegram from Henry C. Gatz, Gatsby's father in Minnesota. Gatz, it seems, learned of Jimmy's (Gatsby's) death through the Chicago newspaper. Gatz refuses to take the body to the Midwest, noting "Jimmy always liked it better down East." That evening, Klipspringer phones and Nick, thinking another mourner will be joining the funeral the next day, is dismayed to learn Klipspringer is only calling to inquire about his tennis shoes. The morning of the funeral, Nick forces his way into Wolfsheim's office, again hoping to convince Gatsby's closest business associate to attend the services. Wolfsheim again refuses, but discloses he did not just give Gatsby a start in business—he made Gatsby's fortune by using him in various questionable activities.

When Nick returns to Gatsby's, he finds Mr. Gatz going through his son's house, growing more proud as he takes in the possessions around him. Pulling out a copy of *Hopalong Cassidy*, once owned by the young Jimmy Gatz, Gatsby's father points out his young son's drive toward self-improvement by calling Nick's attention to the daily schedule penciled in the back. Shortly after, the men adjourn to the funeral. At the graveside are a few servants, the mail carrier, the minister, Nick, and Mr. Gatz. Nick is struck by the bitter injustice of Gatsby's solitary death. Despite all the people who found their way to Gatsby's parties, not one, with the exception of a man known only as "Owl-eyes," bothered to make an appearance at his funeral (and he only made it to the gate after the services ended).

Nick then moves to memories of traveling West when he came home from college. As the train moved further and further West he became more and more comfortable, as if he were returning to a special place just his own. Remembering this memory launches Nick into a discussion of the merits of the Midwest versus the vices of the East. The story is brought to a close when Nick interacts with two people from his past. First, he speaks with Jordan and, although he still feels fondly toward her, he once again coolly dismisses her. Finally, one autumn day, Nick meets Tom along Fifth Avenue. Tom, seeing Nick, makes the first move to speak. Initially Nick refuses to shake Tom's hand, upset with what Tom has come to represent. In the course of their short discussion, Nick learns Tom had a role in Gatsby's death—George Wilson worked his way to the Buchanan house in East Egg and Tom told him who owned the car that struck Myrtle. When Nick leaves, he shakes Tom's hand because he "felt suddenly as though [he] were talking to a child."

The time comes for Nick to leave West Egg and return West. On the last night, he wanders over to Gatsby's for one last visit. Strolling down to the water he is called to remember the way Gatsby's house used to be, filled with people and lavish parties. He considers Gatsby's wonder at picking out Daisy's dock in the darkness, how far Gatsby had traveled in his life, and how he always had hope in the future. In his final thought, Nick links society to the boats eternally moving against the current on the Sound.

Commentary

Theme

The last chapter of *The Great Gatsby* continues a theme begun in the previous chapter, bringing the reader face-to-face with the ugly side of the American dream. Throughout the story, Gatsby has been held up as an example of one who has achieved the American dream—he had money, possessions, independence, and people who wanted to be around him. Or so the reader thinks. Gatsby's funeral takes center stage in this chapter, and with the exception of Nick, who continues to show his moral fiber, what Fitzgerald reveals about the moral decrepitude of those people still living is even worse than any of Gatsby's secrets.

As the chapter opens, Nick tells readers what an impact this course of events makes upon him. "After two years," he writes, "I remember the rest of that day, and that night, and the next day" as a ceaseless string of police officers and newspaper reporters. They came to investigate, and once again, the carnivalesque atmosphere that so often accompanied Gatsby's parties establishes itself. This time, however, the situation is decidedly less merry. Nick, showing he has come to respect Gatsby over the course of the summer, worries that, in fact, the circus-like atmosphere will allow the "grotesque, circumstantial, [and] eager" reporters to mythologize his neighbor, filling the pages of their rags with half-truths and full-blown lies. For Nick, however, even more disturbing than the free-for-all that surrounds the investigation is the fact that he finds himself "on Gatsby's side, and alone."

Nick, by default, assumes the responsibility for making Gatsby's final arrangements, "because no one else was interested—interested . . . with that intense personal interest to which every one has some vague right at the end." Two important things are revealed in that short statement. First, the Nick who is blooming at the end of Chapter 7 has come into fruition in this chapter. He is a man of principles and integrity (which shows more and more as the chapter unfolds). The second idea introduced here is the utter shallowness of the people who, in better times, take every opportunity to be at Gatsby's house, drinking his liquor, eating his food, and enjoying his hospitality, but abandon him at the end: Daisy and Tom have left without a forwarding address. Meyer Wolfsheim, who is "completely knocked down and out" at Gatsby's death, and who wants to "know about the funeral etc." is speaking rhetorically, as his refusal to get involved shows. Even the partygoers disappear. The party is over, and so they move on to the next event, treating their host with the same respect in death that they gave him in life—none at all. Klipspringer is a shining example of all the partygoers when he phones Gatsby's, speaks to Nick, and sidesteps the issue of Gatsby's funeral, shamelessly admitting, "what I called up about was a pair of shoes I left there . . . I'm sort of helpless without them." Nick, again much to his credit, hangs up the phone as Klipspringer tries to leave a forwarding address. The callousness of the people who so eagerly took advantage of Gatsby's hospitality is appalling. Certainly the American dream isn't supposed to end like this, gunned down for something you didn't do, utterly forgotten in your death. Fitzgerald does a fine job of displaying the downside to the American dream and how drive and ambition can, in effect, go too far. Dreams are useful, to a point, but when they consume the dreamer, they lead to destruction.

In true Fitzgerald fashion, and in keeping with the way he has effectively withheld information regarding Gatsby's past throughout the novel, just when the reader thinks he or she knows all, Gatsby's father arrives and gives yet another peek into Gatsby's past. Henry C. Gatz, an unassuming man who is not nearly as wretched as one may have imagined, arrives for his son's burial. The relationship between father and son is estranged, even in death, as evidenced by Gatz's burying "Jimmy" in the East where "he always liked it better." In many ways, Gatz seems a perfectly normal man, yet there is a hint of the superficiality that's similar to Gatsby's former party guests. In one noted example, Nick finds Gatz "walking up and down excitedly in the hall. His pride in his son and in his son's possessions was continually increasing." Apparently Gatz, like so many others, measured Gatsby's merit not on the type of man he was, but on his possessions.

Gatz also fills in Gatsby's early days by pointing to a schedule written in 1906, when Gatsby was about fourteen years old. First, it happens to be in *Hopalong Cassidy*, a famous Western adventure serial from the turn of the century. The book is significant in that it helps explain where Gatsby's dreamer spirit came from. The schedule, too, speaks to a dreamer's spirit. The itinerary is commendable: Gatsby, from the early days, aspired to greatness.

After Gatsby's funeral, wherein Nick and Gatz are the chief (and nearly sole) mourners, little is left for Nick in the East. In fact, he comes to the realization that in the end, Tom, Daisy, Gatsby, Jordan, and he all come from the West and in the end they all "possessed some deficiency in common which made [them] subtly unadaptable to Eastern life." It is only a matter of time before he leaves the East, headed back to the Midwest where, presumably, morality and kindness still exist.

Before he leaves, however, Nick has two important experiences. First, he speaks with Jordan on the phone. What he learns is surprising, but strangely in keeping with her character: She chastises him for being the first man who has ever broken up with her, but before ending the conversation she gets in one last strike, hitting his secret vanity and labeling him as deceitful and dishonest. The second important experience occurs when Nick bumps into Tom on the street. Although he tries to avoid Tom, meeting him can't be helped. Tom, as arrogant as ever, initiates conversation, slightly offended that Nick won't shake hands upon their meeting. During the short conversation, Nick learns that Tom, not surpriingly, had a role in Gatsby's death. When Wilson came to Tom's house, gun in hand, Tom directed Wilson to Gatsby, not feeling an ounce of remorse. In his mind's eye, what he had done was "entirely justified," leading Nick to the apt conclusion that Tom and Daisy were "careless people," using people like objects, until they no longer serve a purpose, then they discard them and move on. This realization is more than Nick can stand and forces him to a new level of maturity. In the end, he shakes hands with Tom, finding no reason not to because Tom (and the people he represents) is really no more than a child.

The final chapter of the novel again draws attention to the green light at the end of the dock, and in turn, to the hopes and dreams of society. Readers are left with a final image of Gatsby as a powerful presence who lives on despite the destruction of the dream and the decay of the estate. Nick again reminds the reader of the thin line separating dreams from reality, causing everyone to stop and wonder about the validity of the dreams people chase. Is everyone, like Gatsby, chasing illusions while neglecting reality? Can anyone ever escape being held hostage by the past, continually working to get back to better times and sometimes missing the joy of the present? According to Nick, the more Gatsby reached for his dream, the more it retreated into the shadowy past, taking him further and further away from what is real. Gatsby had hope and believed in the bounty of what was ahead, but it brought him face-to-face with his own destruction. Although one may look at Gatsby and realize the futility of chasing dreams (at the expense of the here and now), in the end, is anyone really that different? Perhaps there's a bit of Gatsby in everyone. After all, society is, as Nick says, "boats against the current, borne back ceaselessly into the past."

Glossary

pasquinade a satirical piece of writing that holds its object up to ridicule, formerly one posted in a public place; lampoon.

James J. Hill (1838–1916) U.S. railroad magnate and financier; builder of the Great Northern Railway.

Hopalong Cassidy cowboy hero of novelist Clarence E. Mulford's popular western series.

El Greco (about 1541–1614); painter in Italy and Spain.

CHARACTER ANALYSES

The following character analyses delve into the physical, emotional, and psychological traits of the literary work's major characters so that you might better understand what motivates these characters. The writer of this study guide provides this scholarship as an educational tool by which you may compare your own interpretations of the characters. Before reading the character analyses that follow, consider first writing your own short essays on the characters as an exercise by which you can test your understanding of the original literary work. Then, compare your essays to those that follow, noting discrepancies between the two. If your essays appear lacking, that might indicate that you need to re-read the original literary work or re-familiarize yourself with the major characters.

Nick

Nick Carraway, the story's narrator, has a singular place within *The Great Gatsby*. First, he is both narrator and participant. Part of Fitzgerald's skill in *The Great Gatsby* shines through the way he cleverly makes Nick a focal point of the action, while simultaneously allowing him to remain sufficiently in the background. In addition, Nick has the distinct honor of being the only character who changes substantially from the story's beginning to its end. Nick, although he initially seems outside the action, slowly moves to the forefront, becoming an important vehicle for the novel's messages.

On one level, Nick is Fitzgerald's Everyman, yet in many ways he is much more. He comes from a fairly nondescript background. He hails from the upper Midwest (Minnesota or Wisconsin) and has supposedly been raised on stereotypical Midwestern values (hard work, perseverance, justice, and so on). He is a little more complex than that, however. His family, although descended from the "Dukes of Buccleuch," really started when Nick's grandfather's brother came to the U.S. in 1851. By the time the story takes place, the Carraways have only been in this country for a little over seventy years—not long, in the great scope of things. In addition, the family patriarch didn't exhibit the good Midwestern values Nick sees in himself. When the civil war began, Nick's relative "sent a substitute" to fight for him, while he started the family business. This little detail divulges a few things: It places the Carraways in a particular class (because only the wealthy could afford to send a substitute to fight) and suggests that the early Carraways were more tied to commerce than justice. Nick's relative apparently doesn't have any qualms about sending a poorer man off to be killed in his stead. Given this background, it is interesting that Nick would come to be regarded as a level-headed and caring man, enough of a dreamer to set goals, but practical enough to know when to abandon his dreams.

Also contributing to Nick's characterization as an Everyman are his goals in life. He heads East after World War I, seeking largely to escape the monotony he perceives to permeate the Midwest and to make his fortune. He is an educated man who desires more out of life than the quite Midwest can deliver (although it is interesting that before living in the city any length of time he retreats to the country). What helps make Nick so remarkable, however, is the way that he has aspirations without being taken in—to move with the socialites, for example, but not allowing himself to become blinded by the glitz that characterizes their lifestyle. When he realizes what his social superiors are really like (shallow, hollow, uncaring, and self-serving), he is disgusted and, rather than continuing to cater to them, he distances himself. In effect, motivated by his conscience, Nick commits social suicide by forcefully pulling away from people like the Buchanans and Jordan Baker.

In addition to his Everyman quality, Nick's moral sense helps to set him apart from all the other characters. From the first time he interacts with others (Daisy, Tom, and Jordan in Chapter 1), he clearly isn't like them. He is set off as being more practical and down-to-earth than other characters. This essence is again brought to life in Chapter 2 when he doesn't quite know how to respond to being introduced into Tom and Myrtle's secret world (notice, however, that he doesn't feel the need to tell anyone about his adventures). In Chapter 3, again Nick comes off as less mercenary than everyone else in the book as he waits for an invitation to attend one of Gatsby's parties, and then when he does, he takes the time to seek out his host. From these instances (and others like them spread throughout the book) it becomes clear that Nick, in many ways, is an outsider.

Nick has what many of the other characters lack—personal integrity—and his sense of right and wrong helps to elevate him above the others. He alone is repulsed by the phony nature of the socialites. He alone is moved by Gatsby's death. When the other characters scatter to the wind after Gatsby's death, Nick, unable to believe that none of Gatsby's associates will even pay their last respects, picks up the pieces and ensures Gatsby isn't alone in his death. Through the course of *The Great Gatsby* Nick grows, from a man dreaming of a fortune, to a man who knows only too well what misery a fortune can bring.

Gatsby

Like Nick, Gatsby comes from the Midwest (North Dakota, although his father later arrives from Minnesota). Early in the book, he is established as a dreamer who is charming, gracious, and a bit mysterious. As the story unfolds, however, the reader learns more and more what precipitates the mystery: that everything he has done in his adult life has been with the sole purpose of fulfilling the most unrealistic of dreams—to recapture the past. Gatsby is in many ways, as the title suggests, *great*, but when looking at him critically, some of the things he stands for may not be so admirable.

In one sense, Gatsby's rags-to-riches success story makes him an embodiment of the American dream. He started life with little, as the son of fairly unsuccessful farmers. By the time he was a young man he had even less, having voluntarily estranged himself from his family, unable to come to terms with the lot he had been dealt in life. While on his own, he had the opportunity to reinvent himself, and due solely to his own ingenuity, Jimmy Gatz evolved into Jay Gatsby. As such, life became much different (although he was missing one key ingredient: money). He was no longer tied to his early years, but could imagine whatever past for himself he desired. And then he fell in love, a fateful incident that would change the course of his life forever. After meeting Daisy, everything he did was for the singular purpose of winning her. Money was, essentially, the issue that prevented their being together, and so Gatsby made sure he would never again be without it. Gatsby's drive and perseverance in obtaining his goal is, in many senses, commendable. He is a self-made man (in all respects) and as such, is admirable.

However, all positive traits aside, there are aspects of Jay Gatsby that call into question that admiration. Gatsby's money did not come from inheritance, as he would like people to believe, but from organized crime. The story takes place during the time of prohibition and Gatsby has profited greatly from selling liquor illegally. In addition, while people come to Gatsby's parties in droves, he really knows very little about them. In fact, he doesn't *want* to know much about them, just whether they know Daisy. Finally, Gatsby's friendship with Nick really begins to blossom only after he finds out that Nick is Daisy's cousin.

In assessing Gatsby, one must examine his blind pursuit of Daisy. Everything he does, every purchase he makes, every party he throws, is all part of his grand scheme to bring Daisy back into his life for good. In one sense, this is a lovely romantic gesture, but in another sense, it perpetuates a childish illusion. By being so focused on his dream of Daisy, Gatsby moves further and further into a fantasy world. His inability to deal with reality sets him outside the norm and, eventually, has him holding on to the dream leads to his death. By the end of Chapter 7, Gatsby is standing guard outside of Daisy's house on a needless vigil. He is completely unable to realize that his dream is not a reality and so stands watching for a sign from Daisy. He sees what he is doing as noble, honorable, and purposeful. The reader, however, sees the futility of his task as he becomes a parody of his former self. Gatsby is, quite literally, fatally idealistic. He can't wait to distance himself from his past in terms of his family, but yet he lives his adult life trying to recapture the past he had with Daisy. What makes matters worse, too, is that he is in love with the *idea* of Daisy, not Daisy as she herself is.

Daisy

Daisy is *The Great Gatsby*'s most enigmatic, and perhaps most disappointing, character. Although Fitzgerald does much to make her a character worthy of Gatsby's unlimited devotion, in the end she reveals herself for what she really is. Despite her beauty and charm, Daisy is merely a selfish, shallow, and in fact, hurtful, woman. Gatsby loves her (or at least the *idea* of her) with such vitality and determination that readers would like, in many senses, to see her be worthy of his devotion. Although Fitzgerald carefully builds Daisy's character with associations of light, purity, and innocence, when all is said and done, she is the opposite from what she presents herself to be.

From Nick's first visit, Daisy is associated with otherworldliness. Nick calls on her at her house and initially finds her (and Jordan Baker, who is in many ways an unmarried version of Daisy) dressed all in white, sitting on an "enormous couch . . . buoyed up as though upon an anchored balloon . . . [her dress] rippling and fluttering as it [she] had just been blown back in after a short flight around the house." From this moment, Daisy becomes like an angel on earth. She is routinely linked with the color white (a white dress, white flowers, white car, and so on) always at the height of fashion and addressing people with only the most endearing terms. She appears pure in a world of cheats and liars. Given Gatsby's obsession with Daisy and the lengths to which he has gone to win her, she seems a worthy paramour.

As the story continues, however, more of Daisy is revealed, and bit-by-bit she becomes less of an ideal. Given that she is fully aware of her husband's infidelities, why doesn't she do anything about it? Because he has money and power and she enjoys the benefits she receives from these things, she is willing to deal with the affairs. In addition, when she attends one of Gatsby's parties, aside from the half-hour she spends with Gatsby, she has an unpleasant time. She finds the West Egg *nouveaux riches* to be tedious and vulgar, an affront to her "old money" mentality. Another incident that calls Daisy's character into question is the way she speaks of her daughter, Pammy. "I hope she'll be a fool," she says, "that's the best thing a girl can be in this world, a beautiful little fool." Clearly, she has some experience in this area and implies that the world is no place for a woman; the best she can do is hope to survive and the best way to do that is through beauty rather than brains. Later, in Chapter 7 when Pammy makes her only appearance, Daisy treats her like an object, showing her off for guests, suggesting Daisy's lack of concern for her child. Daisy's life revolves around Daisy, allowing Pammy in only when it's convenient. Clearly, in real life Daisy isn't all the way Gatsby remembers—but blinded by his dream, he cannot see the truth.

Although Daisy seems to have found love in her reunion with Gatsby, closer examination reveals that is not at all the case. Although she loves the attention, she has considerations other than love on her mind. First, she knows full well Tom has had affairs for years. Might this not motivate her to get back at him by having an affair of her own? Next, consider Daisy's response to Gatsby's wealth, especially the shirts—does someone in love break into tears upon being shown an assortment of shirts? For Daisy (and Gatsby too, for that matter) the shirts represent wealth and means. When Daisy bows her head and sobs into the shirts, she is displaying her interest in materialism. She doesn't cry because she has been reunited with Gatsby, she cries because of the pure satisfaction all his material wealth brings her. He has become a fitting way in which to get back at Tom. When Tom and Gatsby have their altercation at the hotel in Chapter 7, Daisy's motivations are called into question: Her inability to deny having loved Tom speaks well for her, but at the same time, it suggests that her attachment to Gatsby has been purely business. Tom also knows that after Daisy realizes Gatsby is not of their same social circles, she will return to Tom for the comfort and protection that his money and power bring.

Although Daisy's true self come out more and more each time Nick encounters her, her final actions help show what she has been really made of. When she hits and kills Myrtle Wilson, and then leaves the scene, readers know (as poor Gatsby still does not) that she is void of a conscience. Perhaps all that white that has surrounded her isn't so much purity (although Gatsby, of course, would see it as such), but perhaps the white represents a void, a lack (as in a lack of intellectualism and a lack of conscience). To Daisy, Myrtle is expendable. She is not of the social elite, so what difference does her death make? To add insult to injury, as if she hadn't betrayed Gatsby enough already, she abandons Gatsby in his death. After killing Myrtle, Daisy returns home. She and Tom resolve their differences and leave soon thereafter, moving presumably to another city where they will remain utterly unchanged and life will continue as it always does. Daisy, although ethereal in some qualities, is decidedly devilish in others.

CRITICAL
ESSAYS

On the pages that follow, the writer of this study guide provides critical scholarship on various aspects of Fitzgerald's *The Great Gatsby*. These interpretive essays are intended solely to enhance your understanding of the original literary work; they are supplemental materials and are not to replace your reading of *The Great Gatsby*. When you're finished reading *The Great Gatsby*, and prior to your reading this study guide's critical essays, consider making a bulleted list of what you think are the most important themes and symbols. Write a short paragraph under each bullet explaining why you think that theme or symbol is important; include at least one short quote from the original literary work that supports your contention. Then, test your list and reasons against those found in the following essays. Do you include themes and symbols that the study guide author doesn't? If so, this self test might indicate that you are well on your way to understanding original literary work. But if not, perhaps you will need to re-read *The Great Gatsby*.

Social Stratification: *The Great Gatsby* as Social Commentary

In *The Great Gatsby*, Fitzgerald offers up commentary on a variety of themes—justice, power, greed, betrayal, the American dream and so on. Of all the themes, perhaps none is more well developed than that of social stratification. *The Great Gatsby* is regarded as a brilliant piece of social commentary, offering a vivid peek into American life in the 1920s. Fitzgerald carefully sets up his novel into distinct groups but, in the end, each group has its own problems to contend with, leaving a powerful reminder of what a precarious place the world really is. By creating distinct social classes—old money, new money, and no money—Fitzgerald sends strong messages about the elitism running throughout every strata of society.

The first and most obvious group Fitzgerald attacks is, of course, the rich. However, for Fitzgerald (and certainly his characters), placing the rich all in one group together would be a great mistake. For many of those of modest means, the rich seem to be unified by their money. However, Fitzgerald reveals this is not the case. In *The Great Gatsby*, Fitzgerald presents two distinct types of wealthy people. First, there are people like the Buchanans and Jordan Baker who were born into wealth. Their families have had money for many generations, hence they are "old money." As portrayed in the novel, the "old money" people don't have to work (they rarely, if ever, even speak about business arrangements) and they spend their time amusing themselves with whatever takes their fancy. Daisy, Tom, Jordan, and the distinct social class they represent are perhaps the story's most elitist group, imposing distinctions on the other people of wealth (like Gatsby) based not so much on how much money one has, but where that money came from and when it was acquired. For the "old money" people, the fact that Gatsby (and countless other people like him in the 1920s) has only just recently acquired his money is reason enough to dislike him. In their way of thinking, he can't possibly have the same refinement, sensibility, and taste they have. Not only does he work for a living, but he comes from a low-class background which, in their opinion, means he cannot possibly be like them.

In many ways, the social elite are right. The "new money" people cannot be like them, and in many ways that works in their favor—those in society's highest echelon are not nice people at all. They are judgmental and superficial, failing to look at the essence of the people around them (and themselves, too). Instead, they live their lives in such a way as to perpetuate their sense of superiority—however unrealistic that may be. The people with newly acquired wealth, though, aren't necessarily much better. Think of Gatsby's partygoers. They attend his parties, drink his liquor and eat his food, never once taking the time to even meet their host (nor do they even bother to wait for an invitation, they just show up). When Gatsby dies, all the people who frequented his house every week mysteriously became busy elsewhere, abandoning Gatsby when he could no longer do anything for them. One would like to think the newly wealthy would be more sensitive to the world around them—after all, it was only recently they were without money and most doors were closed to them. As Fitzgerald shows, however, their concerns are largely living for the moment, steeped in partying and other forms of excess.

Just as he did with people of money, Fitzgerald uses the people with no money to convey a strong message. Nick, although he comes from a family with a bit of wealth, doesn't have nearly the capital of Gatsby or Tom. In the end, though, he shows himself to be an honorable and principled man, which is more than Tom exhibits. Myrtle, though, is another story. She comes from the middle class at best. She is trapped, as are so many others, in the valley of ashes, and spends her days trying to make it out. In fact, her desire to move up the social hierarchy leads her to her affair with Tom and she is decidedly pleased with the arrangement. Because of the misery pervading her life, Myrtle has distanced herself from her moral obligations and has no difficulty cheating on her husband when it means that she gets to lead the lifestyle she wants, if only for a little while. What she doesn't realize, however, is that Tom and his friends will never accept her into their circle. (Notice how Tom has a pattern of picking lower-class women to sleep with. For him, their powerlessness makes his own position that much more superior. In a strange way, being with women who aspire to his class makes him feel better about himself and allows him to perpetuate the illusion that he is a good and important man.) Myrtle is no more than a toy to Tom and to those he represents.

Fitzgerald has a keen eye and in *The Great Gatsby* presents a harsh picture of the world he sees around him. The 1920s marked a time of great post-war economic growth, and Fitzgerald captures the frenzy of the society well. Although, of course, Fitzgerald could have no way of foreseeing the stock market crash of 1929, the world he presents in *The Great Gatsby* seems clearly to be headed for disaster. They have assumed skewed worldviews, mistakenly believing their survival lies in stratification and reinforcing social boundaries. They erroneously place their faith in superficial external means (such as money and materialism) while neglecting to cultivate the compassion and sensitivity that, in fact, separate humans from the animals.

In Praise of Comfort: Displaced Spirituality in *The Great Gatsby*

In *The Great Gatsby*, Fitzgerald proudly tackles the theme of spirituality. His attack is subtle, making his message heard most forcefully by what is missing, rather than what is there. The world of *The Great Gatsby* is one of excess, folly, and pleasure, a world where people are so busy living for the moment that they have lost touch with any sort of morality, and end up breaking laws, cheating, and even killing. As debauched as this may sound, however, they have not abandoned spirituality altogether. Rather, Fitzgerald's post-war partiers have substituted materialism and instant creature comforts for philosophic principles, thus suggesting a lack of order and structure in the worlds of East Egg, West Egg, and beyond.

Several elements suggest an imbalance in the moral makeup of the characters found in *The Great Gatsby*. In Nick's opening statements, he is attempting to set himself up as an honorable and trustworthy man. His reason for doing so, however, isn't made entirely clear until readers are introduced to the people with whom he interacts. Barely halfway through the first chapter, Fitzgerald reveals that Tom Buchanan is not only having an affair, but he is shamelessly bold in his refusal to cover it up; his wife knows and although she is a bit irritated, she has come to accept Tom's ways. In addition, those in East Egg discuss things of such great importance as what to do on the longest day and why living in the East is ideal, showing that the supposedly social elite are perhaps a bit out of touch with reality. They clearly treat people as objects, and are unconcerned with whether their actions impede on anyone else's.

After the Buchanans' dinner party, *The Great Gatsby* is again and again filled with excess. In fact, every one of the seven deadly sins (pride, envy, wrath, sloth, avarice, gluttony, and lust) is well represented. None of the characters, including Nick, are free from the deadly devices, which, at least in times past, have traditionally marked the downfall of a community. It is interesting to note that although the seven deadly sins are depicted time and time again by the people in *The Great Gatsby*, the theological counterpart to the seven deadly sins, the seven cardinal virtues (faith, hope, love, prudence, justice, fortitude, and temperance) are nearly invisible. Gatsby, of course, has more hope than all the others put together, but in the end, that one thing, no matter how strong, can't save him.

Although countless acts of questionable integrity can be found within the pages of *The Great Gatsby*, the final and most blatant acts of immorality, of course, come near the book's end. Daisy shows her true self when she runs down Myrtle without even stopping. Gatsby becomes the target for another man's murderous rage when he is gunned down by Wilson (assisted, through association, by Tom). And finally, the last great act of disregard for one's fellow human comes in perhaps the most surprising and disturbing form of all: the lack of mourners at Gatsby's funeral. Despite how people had clamored to be associated with him in life, in death he became useless to them, and so their interests took them elsewhere (with, of course, the sole exception of Nick).

Fitzgerald uses the acts and actions of his characters to convey a sense of growing moral decrepitude, but he compounds his message through other means as well. First, there is the giant billboard, the eyes of Doctor T. J. Eckleburg, which, as George Wilson reveals, represent the eyes of God, which can be interpreted in two ways. On one hand, he could be suggesting that a watchful presence overlooks society all the time, and will hold the world accountable for its actions. Given this interpretation, Fitzgerald seems to be urging readers to remember that they themselves are being watched, so they had better prepare to account for their actions. On the other hand, George's statement may be taken as a testament to his skewed judgment. Has he fallen so far away from standard religion that he does, in fact, believe the enormous eyes watching over the valley of ashes are the eyes of God? Does he interpret the eyes literally, as opposed to metaphorically? If so, Fitzgerald is offering a less uplifting message, suggesting that society has fallen so far away from traditional religious teachings that people have lost all faith and can only misread the significance of the material world around us.

Finally, Fitzgerald uses geography to represent his message of spiritual dysfunction, beginning with the distinct communities of East Egg and West Egg. Granted, their differences are largely socioeconomic, but when looking at the inhabitants of each Egg, the West Eggers stand somewhat above the East Eggers (albeit not by much). Whereas no one in East Egg has any virtues to redeem themselves, West Egg does have Nick, the one character in the book who has a fairly good sense of right and wrong. Just as Fitzgerald favored one Egg over the other (despite it being perceived as the less fashionable Egg), he also pits regions of the country against each other, with similar results. There is no denying that Fitzgerald sees the Midwest as a land of promise. He acknowledges it is less glamorous and exciting than the East, but it has a pureness about it that the East lacks. All his characters come from the Midwest, and in the end, the East does them in. As Nick says, "we possessed some deficiency in common which made us subtly unadaptable to Eastern life." Nick is the only one to realize this, however, and so after he has become completely disillusioned with life in the East, he heads home, presumably to a land that is still connected to the basic tenets of human compassion and charity.

In *The Great Gatsby*, Fitzgerald presents a world in which value systems have gone out of balance. He is not espousing a heavy-handed Christian message, but rather he is encouraging readers to stop and take inventory of their lives. Although some may see Fitzgerald as implying a return to God is necessary for survival, the text supports something far more subtle: Fitzgerald is urging a reconsideration of where society is and where it is going.

CliffsNotes Review

Use this CliffsNotes Review to test your understanding of the original text, and reinforce what you've learned in this book. After you work through the essay questions and useful practice projects, you're well on your way to understanding a comprehensive and meaningful interpretation of *The Great Gatsby*.

Q&A

1. Jay Gatsby's real name is _____ .

2. Dan Cody was important to Gatsby because _____ .

3. Gatsby made his money by _____ .

4. "Old money," "hulking," "aggressive," "confrontational," "infidel," and "racist" all describe _____ .

5. Gatsby is killed by _____ .

6. Myrtle Wilson meets a tragic end when she _____ _____ .

7. Nick Carraway's overarching moral attribute is that he is _____ .

8. Gatsby lives in West Egg, the less fashionable of the Eggs, because _____ .

9. Jordan Baker works as a _____ for a living.

10. People who live in the valley of ashes are haunted by an old billboard of _____ that some characters interpret to be like the eyes of _____ .

Answers: (1) James Gatz. (2) He took Gatsby under his wing and helped him solidify his change from James Gatz to Jay Gatsby. (3) bootlegging/organized crime. (4) Tom Buchanan. (5) George Wilson. (6) runs into the road and is struck and killed by Gatsby's car while Daisy was driving. (7) perhaps the most honest person he knew. (8) it allows him to live across the Sound from Daisy. (9) professional golfer. (10) the eyes of Doctor T. J. Eckelberg; God.

Identify the Quote: Find Each Quote in *The Great Gatsby*

1. "They're a rotten crowd," I shouted across the lawn. "You're worth the whole damn bunch put together."

2. "So we beat on, boats against the current, borne back ceaselessly into the past."

3. "When the *Jazz History of the World* was over, girls were putting their heads on men's shoulders in a puppyish, convivial way, girls were swooning backward playfully into men's arms, even into groups, knowing that some one would arrest their falls—but no one swooned backward on Gatsby, and no French bob touched Gatsby's shoulder, and no singing quartets were formed with Gatsby's head for one link."

4. "He had changed since his New Haven years. Now he was a sturdy straw-haired man of thirty with a rather hard mouth and a supercilious manner. Two shining arrogant eyes had established dominance over his face and gave him the appearance of always leaning aggressively forward. Not even the effeminate swank of his riding clothes could hide the enormous power of that body—he seemed to fill those glistening boots until he strained the top lacing, and you could see a great pack of muscle shifting when his shoulder moved under his thin coat."

5. "[When the nurse told me I had] a girl, I turned my head away and wept. 'All right,' I said, 'I'm glad it's a girl. And I hope she'll be a fool—that's the best thing a girl can be in this world, a beautiful little fool."

Answers: (1) Nick Carraway, upon realizing exactly what Tom, Daisy, and Jordan represent. (2) Nick's final lines in the book. (3) Nick's description of one of Gatsby's parties is telling primarily for the way it shows how Gatsby, despite being the host, remains distant from his guests. (4) Nick Carroway giving his impression of Tom Buchanan. (5) This is one of the few things Daisy says about her daughter, and it is a telling remark: She herself is a good embodiment of the "beautiful little fool."

Essay Questions

1. The notion of the American dream figures prominently in this story. How should readers define "American dream"? Morevoer, is pursuing the American dream necessarily a good thing, as evidenced by *The Great Gatsby*?

2. Explore the character of Nick. How are readers supposed to feel about him? In what ways does he come off as reliable or unreliable?

3. Fitzgerald's story shows the clear delineations between different strata of society: new money, old money, some money, and no money. How are readers to interpret his comments on each of these groups? Does he hold any one group above the other? Are there ways in which people of all groups are alike?

4. Throughout the story, Gatsby has difficulty accepting that the past is over and done with. Where do you find evidence of his trying to recapture the past? What does this say about him? Should people live their lives yearning for something in the past? Why or why not?

5. Part of Fitzgerald's strength as a writer comes from his imagistic style. His writing is very sensory-oriented. What examples of sensory-oriented imagery (sight, taste, touch, smell, sound) can you find in the story? What kind of atmosphere do these details help create? How do they affect you as a reader?

6. It is not uncommon to hear the term "a self-made man." In what possible ways might this term be explained? How does Gatsby fit that definition? In what ways does he take it too literally?

7. Although Gatsby professed to love Daisy, there is a sense that he was not in love with her as much as he was in love with the *idea* of her. Where can you find evidence of Gatsby's devotion to an ideal rather than an actual person?

8. Although Nick Carraway has his reservations about Gatsby, it is clear he thinks of him fondly; after all, he titles the book *The Great Gatsby*. He leads a questionable existance and comes to a tragic end, yet Nick (and by extension, the readers) feel empathetic toward him. Does Gatsby deserve to be called "Great"? In what ways is he great? In what ways is he not? In the end, which wins out: greatness or mediocrity?

Practice Projects

1. Design an electronic study guide on the Internet for *The Great Gatsby*. Include useful background information on Fitzgerald and the book itself, as well as discussions of key themes found in *The Great Gatsby*. Link to other Fitzgerald resources, as well as sites that provide key historical background on things such as the Jazz Age, the Lost Generation, Prohibition, and so on.

2. Take on the persona of one of the characters and write a short essay introducing yourself to others. What are you like? What motivates you? What are your goals? Use ample textual details in creating your answer.

3. Write a short play of one of the scenes in *The Great Gatsby* (perhaps Tom and Myrtle at the apartment or Daisy and Gatsby at Nick's for tea). Using dialogue, work on capturing the essence of the characters, as well as the scene's significance.

4. Are there modern parallels for Gatsby, Daisy, Nick, and the rest? Is our society like or unlike the Jazz Age society depicted in Fitzgerald's novel?

5. Explore the critical reception of Fitzgerald's work. Initially *The Great Gatsby* was far less successful than his first novel, *This Side of Paradise*. Why? When did *The Great Gatsby* begin to win fame and take its place among great twentieth century American works?

6. How does *The Great Gatsby* compare with other Fitzgerald novels, for example, in comparison to *This Side of Paradise*, *The Beautiful and Damned*, or *The Last Tycoon*.

7. In what ways is *The Great Gatsby* an autobiographical novel? Where can you find evidence of Fitzgerald in the work? Should these self-reflective references matter or should the work be judged solely as a work of fiction? What are the benefits and drawbacks of imposing biographical criticism on this work?

8. Using microfilm, microfiche, and the Internet (as well as books and traditional print media), research some of the historical happenings of the 1920s. Go back and reconstruct what life was like during Fitzgerald's time. Examine newspapers from the '20s (microfilm is likely to be your best bet) and make a list of what made news. Based on your findings, how accurate was Fitzgerald in capturing the frenzy of life in the 1920s? Were his reflections about all groups of people—the rich, the middle class, and the poor—accurate or far-fetched?

9. Create a visual representation of the story (a painting, a sculpture, a photo, a film, a dance). What colors, textures, and symbols will help you capture the essence of this story?

10. The opera version of *The Great Gatsby* premiered in 1999. Using the resources available to you, trace the opera's reception. What can you find out about the opera? How well received was it? Is *The Great Gatsby* a good candidate for a contemporary opera? Why or why not?

11. Join one of the many listservs or Internet discussion forums dedicated to Fitzgerald. Expand your understanding of the text while helping others to see your point of view.

CliffsNotes Resource Center

The learning doesn't need to stop here. CliffsNotes Resource Center shows you the best of the best—links to the best information in print and online about the author and/or related works. And don't think that this is all we've prepared for you; we've put all kinds of pertinent information at www.cliffsnotes.com. Look for all the terrific resources at your favorite bookstore or local library and on the Internet. When you're online, make your first stop www.cliffsnotes.com where you'll find more incredibly useful information about *The Great Gatsby*.

Books

This CliffsNotes book, published by Houghton Mifflin Harcourt, provides a meaningful interpretation of The Great Gatsby. If you are looking for information about the author and/or related works, check out these other publications:

BAUGHMAN, JUDITH S. AND MATTHEW JOSEPH BRUCCOLI, eds. *F. Scott Fitzgerald: A Life in Letters.* New York: Scribner, 1994.

BRUCCOLI, MATTHEW J., ed. *New Essays on the Great Gatsby* (American Novel Series). Cambridge: Cambridge UP, 1991.

KUEHL, JOHN AND JACKSON R. BRYER, eds. *Dear Scott, Dear Max: The Fitzgerald-Perkins Correspondence.* New York: Simon & Schuster, 1991.

MEYERS, JEFFREY. *Scott Fitzgerald.* 1994. New York: Cooper Square Press, 2000.

TATE, MARY JO AND MATTHEW J. BRUCCOLI. *F. Scott Fitzgerald A to Z.* Checkmark Books, 1999.

TREDELL, NICHOLAS, ed. *F. Scott Fitzgerald: The Great Gatsby* (Columbia Critical Guides). New York: Columbia UP, 1999.

It's easy to find books published by Houghton Mifflin Harcourt. You'll find them in your favorite bookstores (on the Internet and at a store near you). We also have two web sites that you can use to read about all the books we publish:

- www.cliffsnotes.com
- www.dummies.com

Video

The Great Gatsby. Dir. Jack Clayton. Perf. Robert Redford, Mia Farrow, Sam Waterston, and Bruce Dern. Paramount, 1974.

Internet

Check out these Web resources for more information about *The Great Gatsby* and F. Scott Fitzgerald:

F. Scott Fitzgerald Centenary, http://www.sc.edu/fitzgerald/index.html—a repository, sponsored by the University of South Carolina, for a vast variety of information regarding Fitzgerald's life and career, including a few voice and film clips.

Our Side of Paradise, http://www.pioneerplanet.com/archive/fitzgerald/—designed by the *St. Paul Pioneer Press* to honor the city's native son on his centenary and provides links to feature stories on Fitzgerald's work and his life, especially as it links to St. Paul. Regardless of where you live, be sure to take a tour of Fitzgerald's haunts in St. Paul, Minnesota by visiting the tour link. If you live in the area or are visiting, consider doing the walk in person. If that's not an option, follow the links for a virtual tour.

The Great Gatsby: Q & A, http://www.schirmer.com/composers/harbison_gatsby_qa.html—devoted to John Harbison's opera version of *The Great Gatsby*, which was commissioned by the Metropolitan Opera and debuted in 1999. It takes an interesting look at how a novel becomes adapted for an opera, as well as what it was about the novel that made the transition likely. This site also provides links to other related resources.

Next time you're on the Internet, don't forget to drop by www.cliffsnotes.com. We've created an online Resource Center that you can use today, tomorrow, and beyond.

Index